PSYCHOLOGY AND AMERICA'S URBAN DILEMMAS

D0807130

WITHDRAWN

Psychology and the Problems of Society

Kenneth J. Gergen, Consulting Editor
Swarthmore College

Ashmore and McConahay:
Psychology and America's Urban Dilemmas

Kidder and Stewart:
The Psychology of Intergroup Relations
Conflict and Consciousness

Pizer and Travers:
Psychology and Social Change

PSYCHOLOGY AND AMERICA'S URBAN DILEMMAS

Richard D. Ashmore
Department of Psychology
Livingston College, Rutgers University

John B. McConahay
Departments of Political Science and Psychology
Yale University

McGraw-Hill Book Company

New York/St. Louis/San Francisco/Düsseldorf/Johannesburg
Kuala Lumpur/London/Mexico/Montreal/New Delhi/Panama
Paris/São Paulo/Singapore/Sydney/Tokyo/Toronto

Psychology and America's Urban Dilemmas

234567890BPBP798765

This book was set in Press Roman by Allen Wayne Technical
Corp. The editor was Richard R. Wright,
the cover was designed by J. E. O'Connor;
the cover illustration by Cathy Hull;
the production supervisor was Milton J. Heiberg.
The Book Press, Inc., was printer and binder.

Library of Congress Cataloging in Publication Data

Ashmore, Richard D
  Psychology and America's urban dilemmas.

  (Psychology and the problems of society)
  Includes bibliographical references.
  1. Cities and towns--United States. 2. Social
problems. I. McConahay, John B., joint author.
II. Title.
HT167.A85   301.36'3'0973   74-9519
ISBN 0-07-002453-7

Contents

Foreword

The present volume represents a milestone in the development of the psychological sciences. Until the present time there has been no psychology of urban problems. There are no psychological journals devoted to the problems of the city, no research institutes with the city as the prime focus, no recognized core literature, and no foundation specifically designated for research on urban problems. In view of this, it may well be asked how a book can be written on the psychology of urban problems. Richard Ashmore and John McConahay have not only written such a book, but in so doing they have essentially created the field.

The field of urban psychology, as envisioned by the present authors, is a rich and exciting one—both informative in its present perspectives and challenging in its potential. At the outset the authors make no claims for the superiority of the psychological perspective in understanding urban problems. In fact, the entire supposition that various disciplines should compete for superiority in understanding is eschewed. Rather, Ashmore and McConahay convincingly demonstrate the necessity for cooperative, interdisciplinary efforts. They reveal the shortcomings of considering the psychology of the individual without reference to the large-scale social systems in which he is enmeshed; they illustrate the importance of taking into account the historical antecedents of contemporary city life; and they demonstrate the necessity of viewing psychological processes as wholly intertwined with political, legal, economic, or educational factors.

The authors' view of the field is also one which encompasses diverse methodologies. While most areas of psychology are committed to the laboratory experiment as the major means of assaying reality, Ashmore and McConahay make a strong case for using multiple methodologies. Since tackling the problems of the city requires a good deal of first-hand observation, the laboratory is not the place to begin research on such problems. The laboratory serves primarily as an ancillary method which is most fruitful when used to demonstrate causality among factors. The examination of historical documents, cross-cultural assessments, public records, and the results of public opinion surveys are also advocated. It is suggested that in certain cases even the study of animal colonies may play an important role in fathoming the problems of city life.

Finally, it is important to note that Ashmore and McConahay envision this developing field as a fundamentally applied one. Ideally both the development of theory and the collection of data should germinate from the critical problems that face the city dweller, and the final result should be concrete programs of ameliorative action. Ashmore and McConahay are willing to suggest avenues of change. They are quite aware that all "the facts are never in," and are willing to assess the evidence at hand and to offer "best solutions" given the present state of knowledge.

It is a pleasure to welcome the present volume into the world of social inquiry.

Kenneth J. Gergen
Professor and Chairman
Department of Psychology
Swarthmore College

Preface

When they are mentioned at all in a book about social problems, such matters as the authors' values, what motivated them to write the book, and what problems will be covered or excluded are usually examined in the preface, where they are frequently read by the professor, but only rarely by the student. It is our firm conviction, however, that discussions of social problems are only meaningful when the reader is aware of the value context in which they are written. Therefore, we have included an explicit statement of our values, motives, and criteria for topic selection in the first chapter in order to make it an integral part of the book. As a consequence, this preface will be very brief.

Every book requires the help of both institutions and individuals and this one is no exception. We want to thank Wendy Ashmore, Frances Del Boca, Fred Grupp, Peter Lupsha, Cynthia Margolin, and especially Kenneth Gergen for reading earlier drafts of the manuscript and making suggestions that did much to improve the final work. Wendy Graetz, Diane Straus, and Ruthann Theodore provided invaluable bibliographic and other research assistance for which we are very thankful. Frances Del Boca, Jill Grubb, and Joyce Kowalewski did excellent jobs typing and editing the several drafts. We also want to thank the following institutions for their financial support. Rutgers University Research Council for a grant to Richard Ashmore, and Yale University's Center for the Study of the City of the Institution for Social and Policy Studies for a grant to John McConahay. Additional support was received from the National Institute of Mental Health in conjunction with its grant to Yale University (MH-11526), Advanced Training in Psychology for Political Scientists, John B. McConahay, Director.

Finally, we wish to extend special thanks to Wendy Ashmore and Shirley Frey-McConahay and to John Edward, Susan Marie, and Mary Katherine McConahay.

Richard D. Ashmore   John B. McConahay

Chapter 1

Where We're At...
and Hope to Take You

In the spring of 1971 a national sample of Americans was asked what fears they had for the United States (Cantril & Roll, 1971). Although "war" was the number one fear of those polled, there was much concern expressed about affairs at home. Among the most frequently mentioned national worries were "national disunity, political instability" (for example, conflicts between blacks and whites, rich and poor, young and old), "economic instability, inflation," "lack of law and order," "pollution," "drugs," "racial tensions," and "unemployment." Thus, Americans were—and, we think, continue to be—quite worried about domestic affairs. And, many of the problems that concern them are most prevalent in urban areas (e.g., racial tensions) or derive from urbanization itself (e.g., pollution). This book is designed to cover psychological research and theory relevant to understanding and, hopefully, alleviating some of the major urban dilemmas confronting the United States.

This first chapter, which sets the stage for our discussion of specific urban problems, is divided into three parts. First, we will try to elucidate our personal values and attitudes ("where we're at") so that you, the reader, can take these into account when reading the remaining chapters. Then we will define what a city is and discuss the historical context of contemporary American cities. And, finally, we will briefly outline the contents of the remainder of this book and present the rationale for its organization ("where we hope to take you").

WHERE WE'RE AT

"Why is a statement of your values and attitudes necessary? I thought you [the authors] were simply supposed to present the scientific 'facts' and discuss their implications." We think there are two major reasons why such a statement is necessary, even mandatory. First, scientific study doesn't automatically produce "facts," especially when the object of study is human behavior. Psychology is concerned with uncovering the laws or principles governing human behavior, which it does by studying *observables.* But even when regularities in observables are noticed (e.g., under conditions X most people will do Y), and a particular explanation fits the data, there is no assurance that the explanation is correct. That is, empirical research does not prove particular theories or validate particular explanations but, rather, disproves those that do not fit the data. The theory or explanation we subscribe to at any given time must be held tentatively because further research may find it partially or completely wrong.

Second, room for interpretation is greater when we are dealing with research on social problems, since data are scarce (e.g., the effects of problems such as crowding have just recently come under careful scientific study) and generally there are conflicting findings (e.g., some investigators find one relationship, others another). Because of these difficulties—disallowance of definitive "proof," scarcity of data on social problems, and conflicting results—a lot of room is left for interpretation of the *meaning* of the results of scientific investigations.

This is not to say that we downgrade the scientific study of social problems. To the contrary, we feel that such study is necessary, and potentially helpful. Its value, however, is not that it proves facts but rather that (1) it encourages objective consideration of explanations (i.e., no matter how strongly we dislike a finding, we must accept it if it has been established by methodologically sound empirical research), and (2) the scientific study of social problems is by its very nature open to public scrutiny and, thus, faulty methods and findings can be caught and corrected.

As we hope to show at several points throughout this book, humans are influenced by their values and attitudes in their interpretation of "reality." For example, a national sample of adults was interviewed following the first television debate in 1960 between Nixon and Kennedy. They were asked who their predebate presidential choice was and who they thought won the debate. Most of those who favored Kennedy felt he won, most of those who were undecided felt neither man won, while Nixon supporters generally believed he won (Katz & Feldman, 1962). In sum, political persuasion strongly influenced how the debate was perceived. We, too, are subject to the same value and attitude influences on how we interpret reality; consequently, we feel obliged to let you know where we stand on certain issues.

In terms of political and economic persuasion, we would be classified by most as "white middle-class liberals," although a former Vice President of the United States labeled people like us "effete snobs." Our liberalism has three aspects that are relevant to the writing of this book. First, we are primarily reformers rather than revolutionaries. We see much wrong with the American socioeconomic and political structure, but we approach the task of making changes from "within the system" rather than from outside it (even though the changes we propose in ensuing chapters would certainly alter that system significantly). Second, we see humans as being as capable of doing good as of doing evil. War, genocide, discrimination, and so on are so common that people seem almost to be afflicted by some "original sin" as part of their genetic make-up. We do not, however, believe that evil behavior is biologically determined, and thus inevitable. Rather, we see most social problems as due largely to environmental factors and consequently amenable to change. The third aspect of our liberal value-attitude structure is the belief that America should foster cultural pluralism through both the attitudes and values of its citizens *and* the operation of public institutions. The concept of the American melting pot—people of different languages, colors, religions, etc. coming to live in America and gradually assimilating the "American way of life"—has long dominated popular thinking about the various cultural groups that make up the American populace. Our view is that the melting pot goal is neither possible (cf. Gordon, 1964) nor desirable. We see cultural pluralism as a better goal, although it is certainly not one easily achieved. In the ideal case of a culturally pluralistic society, the constituent groups share some common values and attitudes while retaining certain cultural attributes that define their own uniqueness. All individuals and cultural groups are valued because they are all equally human; one's unique cultural heritage is valued because it helps to define one's sense of self. In short, we favor a society that would accept and promote subcultural differences rather than a melting pot society in which parts of one's cultural heritage must be discarded in order to gain acceptance.

We also feel strongly that psychology has too often couched the study of social problems in terms of the traits of individuals rather than in terms of the functioning of social institutions. For example, psychologists have most often studied the social problem of crime by assessing the personality traits and attitudes of those labeled by society as criminal; they have also attempted to study intergroup hostility by looking primarily at the attributes of individuals ("prejudice," "authoritarian personality structure," and so on). In part this emphasis derives from psychology's role as the science of individual human behavior, while sociology, political science, anthropology, and economics concentrate on the behavior of larger social groupings. However, to explain human behavior without reference to the larger social context in which it occurs is often to misinterpret that behavior. Therefore, in this book we shall stress the role of societal and institutional influences on human behavior. At points, we shall underplay the role of individual-level factors, as we feel that they have been amply discussed elsewhere. However, in our focus on broad social influences, we shall be especially sensitive to their psychological underpinnings and implications.

An important by-product of focusing on the individual in discussing social problems is that the individual has been seen as the problem. For example, up to the mid-1960s the conflict between blacks and whites in this country was termed the "Negro problem." In other words, the victims were seen as the problem. We feel that much the same thing has occurred in the treatment of school failure by ghetto children and of poverty itself. Consequently, our consideration of these topics will focus on sociostructural and institutional factors. At times we may go too far in this stress (although we don't think so) and the reader should be aware that some psychologists would certainly disagree with us. (We shall refer the reader to these other researchers where appropriate.)

Our stress on structural and institutional factors in the etiology of various urban problems leads us to propose changes in these structures to help alleviate the problems. The reader should not conclude that we think such changes can be easily made, or implemented exactly as planned. Institutional changes are difficult to make, and, unless very carefully studied, many changes that are good in theory can be disastrous in practice. Most social problems have several "causes" and no single change will eradicate the problem. Finally, a change intended to reduce one problem often increases another since social structures are intricately intertwined.

Most social problems have multiple and complex sources; nevertheless, the usual approach is for someone to propose a single solution which must then be sold to the people and/or the government. So much effort is generally devoted to convincing people that one particular solution is the best approach (often implying it is the *only* approach) that once it is implemented its proponents cannot admit to themselves or others that they might have been wrong. This is a consequence we wish to avoid. Our commitment is to solving urban problems, not to promoting a particular solution or a particular political ideology. We would like to see an experimenting society such as Donald Campbell (1969) has proposed: one that seeks solutions to problems, uses the best possible method of evaluating the effects of a given solution and, most importantly, is willing to try a new approach if the first one fails. Thus, though we shall be suggesting certain changes, they are offered in this attitude of experimentation. Given the level of information available to us, they are the best approaches we know of. However, new information or evaluations of new programs may lead to other suggestions.

That we see structural changes as necessary, yet difficult to implement properly, has made writing this book quite painful. At times we thought, "We really know something about why X condition exists" and "The need to change this particular aspect of institutional functioning is clear." But the political and practical difficulties in achieving such changes often seemed equally clear. Consequently, researching and writing this book was accompanied by alternating periods of optimism ("we have something important to say") and pessimism ("it won't make any difference"). Hopefully this book will make a difference.

THE HISTORICAL CONTEXT OF THE CONTEMPORARY AMERICAN CITY

In order to understand better the specific urban problems discussed in later chapters, we feel that you, the reader, should not only be aware of our attitudes and values but should also have some understanding of how and why American cities have developed the way they have. Therefore, we shall make a brief detour at this point to outline the chronological development of cities and discuss current trends relevant to American cities.

What Is a City?

This is a deceptively simple question. We all have a feeling that certain entities are cities while others are not, but it is difficult to specify what characteristics define a city and there is no overwhelming consensus among social scientists. Many emphasize the size or the density of the population in a particular area. Others stress physical or visual features such as tall buildings and man-made environments. Still, others base their definition of a city upon the nature of the economic activities that are found in an area. Finally, some social scientists rely upon an intuitive definition; like pornography, they can't define it, but they know it when they see it (Tager & Goist, 1970).

Thus, there is much disagreement among those concerned with cities about exactly what they are studying. For our purposes, we shall use the following as a preliminary working definition: ". . . a city [is] a relatively large, dense and permanent settlement of socially heterogeneous individuals" (Wirth, 1970, p. 119). If we add to this general definition the fact that the functions of cities have been different in different historical periods we can describe cities of any particular age reasonably well by combining the general features of largeness, density, and social heterogeneity with knowledge about the functions of cities at that particular time. We will now turn to a brief discussion of the various functions that cities have served through history.

Preindustrial Cities

During their earliest stage of development people depended upon hunting and gathering of food for survival. Hence, they lived in small groups that were frequently on the move. With the advent of agriculture and the domestication of animals, however, people became more settled, and the earliest cities were developed in order to protect accumulated agricultural and other products from outsiders. Not only were these early cities defensive positions; they were also centers of commerce and political organization. Although the cities of ancient Greece and Rome, of Medieval Europe, and of the Renaissance differed from one another in many specifics, no fundamental change in cities took place until the advent of the industrial revolution.

The Industrial City

In the late 1700s and early 1800s technological advances—particularly the harnessing of inanimate sources of energy (first water, then steam, and later gas and oil)—converted the United States and certain Western European nations into manufacturing rather than agricultural societies. Cities became centers of production, with factories, not storehouses, as their focal points. The industrial city quickly became a strong magnet, attracting farmers by opportunities for material advancement and by the sheer excitement that population centers possess. At the same time, advances in agricultural technology reduced the need for farm labor and therefore served to push farmers off the land. Together these complementary forces produced a mass migration to urban areas.

The American Industrial City

Although urbanization in America was under way by the early 1800s, the availability of land (the "open frontier") served to check the growth of industrial cities until the Civil War produced a great need for manufactured goods. The 1880s saw a huge migration to urban areas and, by 1900, the increase in the urban population was over seven times as great as the increase in the rural population (Tager & Goist, 1970, p. 2).

The rapid, large-scale growth of cities led to many problems, among them severe overcrowding and a paucity of adequate housing. Many large cities, in fact, were surrounded by shantytowns where the inhabitants lived in makeshift lean-tos. City services were totally inadequate: fires burned unchecked, water was often polluted, garbage collection and sewage services were unreliable, and so on. Clearly, many of our contemporary urban dilemmas are not new phenomena.

Suburbanization of American Society

In the early years of industrialization in the United States, the lack of large-scale transportation systems meant that workers had to live in huge tenements built close to the factories. With the advent of railroads, however, workers were able to live farther from inner-city areas. This resulted in the development of America's earliest "suburbs," which were built along railroad lines.

In the 1920s the automobile ushered in a new era of urban development. The car made it possible for those working in the city to live at quite a distance from both the city itself and from rail lines. Thus, after 1920, suburbanization began on a wide scale. Although this trend was held up by the Depression of the 1930s and by World War II, the suburbs have grown at an astounding pace since 1946. In fact, in 1970, more Americans lived in suburban areas (76 million persons) than in central cities (64 million persons) (Taeuber, 1972, p. 774).

Ethnic and Racial Migrations to the City

Although the industrial revolution succeeded because it was able to harness inanimate energy sources, most early manufacturing still required much human labor. The earlier factories, in fact, thrived on the huge supply of cheap labor provided by the already overcrowded (and still growing) cities. The large numbers of immigrants (particularly Irish, Jewish, and Italian) drawn to the United States around the turn of the century helped maintain this pool, since the latest arrivals, being in the greatest need, would work for the lowest wages.

As these European immigrants gained political and economic power, they joined the movement to the suburbs that began in the 1920s. This exodus was accelerated by the second great migration experienced by the United States: the migration of Southern rural blacks to the cities. This last wave of migration has had a profound effect upon contemporary American cities; it will be discussed in detail in Chapter 6.

WHERE WE HOPE TO TAKE YOU

Now that you have some idea of our ideological leanings and of the historical background of the contemporary American city, we would like to summarize briefly the contents of the rest of this book.

The next six chapters are devoted to specific urban problems, which are grouped into three sections: the twin problems of too much and too little, the failure of two of the city's major institutions, and race relations in the city. This organization is meant to highlight what we feel to be the underlying structure of the city's problems: (1) the scarcity of resources (including space) and the difficulty in allocating them properly; (2) the inadequacies of existing formal, collective (i.e., institutional) means of dealing with this situation; and (3) the intricate relation between race relations and urban problems.

In Chapters 2 and 3, we will discuss two general sets of problems intrinsic to modern-day American cities. Traditionally, cities are where the action is (employment as well as entertainment and cultural stimulation) and people tend to head toward action. Thus, crowding is intimately bound up with the drawing power of urban areas. And where people are, so, too, are their products and by-products, so that cities are further characterized by the various noxious elements we call pollution: too much noise, too much garbage in the streets, sewage in the water, and smoke and automobile emissions in the air.

Following the discussion of the psychological effects of crowding and pollution in Chapter 2, we shall turn in Chapter 3 to the problems of too little. Although central city areas have been declining slightly in population, Americans continue to move to urban areas. Most leave farms and other rural settings in order to find a better, more stable job, and hence a happier life style, in and around the cities. But for many, particularly the poor and nonwhite, this hope is not fulfilled. What was once rural poverty is increasingly becoming an urban problem as the exodus to urban areas continues.

In the next section (Chapters 4 and 5) we discuss two of the institutions designed to serve urban dwellers. Although many such institutions could be singled out for analysis (e.g., housing, transportation, health) we chose education and the criminal justice system because they occupy central positions in the total picture of urban problems. Education is a major source of upward mobility in our society, and only if schools operate fairly and efficiently can the American credo of equal opportunity become a reality. In Chapter 4 we present evidence that, at present, the schools serving ghetto communities are not operating fairly and efficiently. Chapter 5 is concerned with the parallel problems of inequity in judicial proceedings.

The final section of the book is concerned with black-white relations in the cities. While intergroup conflict is certainly not restricted to urban areas, race relations and urban problems are intimately bound together. For example, in Chapters 3 and 4 we will see that the problems of poverty and school failure are more likely to impinge on nonwhites. In the final section, however, we look directly at race relations: Chapter 6 discusses the attitudes and motives of urban blacks, while Chapter 7 is concerned with parallel phenomena among white Americans.

The above topics pretty well cover what people think of as urban problems, with two possible exceptions: drugs and crime.[1] We have not discussed these topics for three reasons. First (and least important), neither of us is well acquainted with the research literature on these topics. Second, the literature that we are familiar with indicates that both problems are multifaceted and are far from restricted to urban environs. According to Clausen (1971, p. 204), although heroin use is primarily a problem of inner-city slum areas, hallucinogens (e.g., LSD) are more often found in "student, 'hippie,' and intellectual circles," and other drugs (e.g., marijuana) are used almost everywhere. The same cloudy picture emerges in considering crime. Most of us think of crime in terms of "crime in the streets": a dirty, violent criminal sneaking up behind the unsuspecting "good citizen," whacking him over the head, and stealing his money (see our discussion on crime in

---

[1] For research and theory concerning drugs see Clausen (1971), and Davis (1972); for excellent sociopsychological discussions of crime see Cohen & Short (1972), Cressy & Ward (1969).

Chapter 5). Official crime statistics (e.g., police arrest records) have tended to support this image since such crime rates are higher for inner-city, low socioeconomic status blacks than for other groups. But several studies of the 1960s suggested that there were rather large discrepancies between number of crimes committed and arrests made *and* that the discrepancies often tended to *overestimate* the crime rate of lower socioeconomic status individuals. Also, the crime-in-the-streets image leaves out altogether the white-collar criminal.

But the final, and most important, reason that crime and drugs are not discussed is that we see these as second-order or derivative problems. Specifically, we see drug abuse and crime as adaptations to social and personal circumstances. In the case of the ghetto dweller, these circumstances involve living in a dirty, noisy environment, having to worry continually about having enough money to survive, being discriminated against, and so on. We will direct our attention in the remaining chapters to those conditions that we feel are the primary or first-order problems of cities.

Chapter 2

The City Has Too Much

The Harvard mathematician and traveling bard, Tom Lehrer, gave the following Calypso warning to those who might find themselves visiting or living in the cities of the United States:

If you visit American city,
You will find it very pretty
Just two things of which you must beware:
Don't drink the water and don't breathe the air.[1]

Foul air and bad water are not the only afflictions of our cities, however. Cities are too crowded, too noisy, and have too few resources to care for all of their citizens. In this chapter, we shall look at the things that cities have too much of: people, and air and noise pollution, in particular. In the next chapter we shall examine the problems of too little—poverty, welfare, and hunger.

[1] Taken from *Tom Lehrer's Second Song Book* by Tom Lehrer, © 1968 by Crown Publishers, Inc. Used by permission.

A BRIEF RETURN TO THE JUNGLE

We begin our examination of the city's problems by looking first at animals in their natural settings. This is not as preposterous as it first appears because human beings, products of evolution that they are, may possibly still bear some primitive biological or genetically transmitted mechanism that determines how they respond to crowding. Such mechanisms, which once may have helped humans adapt to their environment, may be springing forth to haunt us today in our crowded cities.

Malthus and other early students of population dynamics assumed that population growth in a given species was limited by its ability to produce or secure food. But population control by starvation would be a rather ineffective evolutionary mechanism for ensuring the survival of a given species whether that species were the lemming, the monkey, or the human. If that were the only process, all the available food might be consumed before starvation could eliminate sufficient members of the group to enable it to adjust its population level to that of the food supply. Thus, while the availability of food during the leanest years might have set the extreme upper limit upon population size, those species that survived over the long haul must have developed mechanisms for population control that were activated well before the critical food supply point was reached.

Research with animals has suggested what these mechanisms might be. In a classic experiment (Calhoun, 1962), Norway rats were allowed to multiply freely in an enclosed area, a fixed amount of space. Calhoun and his assistants saw to it that there was always more than enough food and water available for all the rats, no matter how many there were. Under these circumstances, the rat population reached levels of density never seen in natural settings.

Following this population explosion strange behaviors began to emerge in the rat colony. Some rats became extremely aggressive while others scarcely moved at all. More importantly for the present point, the rats' sexual behavior changed dramatically. Some became sexual "deviates" and others became hyperactive heterosexuals. Female rats lost interest in their young, while males destroyed nests. Infant mortality increased and the number of successful pregnancies decreased. Some adults died of no apparent cause and others appeared to have mental breakdowns. Thus, the population of rats, even though food and water were always plentiful, declined drastically in a very short period.

Some male rats managed to occupy certain spaces in the cage, which they defended against the others, and in these areas behavior remained as before; but the majority of the rats who were crowded into the central areas exhibited the behaviors described above. Thus, where there was aggressive competition, it was for space, not food, water, or sex.

Beginning about ten years before Calhoun, Christian (1963) performed autopsies on a broad spectrum of animals in natural settings in which competition for space had occurred. He presented striking evidence that, in mammals at least, the stress of the competition produced pathologies in the endocrine feedback mechanisms that led to behavior (and sometimes to death) in animals that were otherwise normal and healthy.

The net result in both the Calhoun and Christian studies was a reduction in the animal population long before the available food supply would have been threatened. Hence, one explanation for the behavior of the animals is that some survival mechanism had been triggered in order to reduce the population before mass starvation could threaten the entire species (Brown, 1965).

Both Calhoun and Christian were very cautious about generalizing to humans from their work with animals, but the temptation to do just that is very powerful. After all, people are mammals and the products of evolution. Is it not possible that, as we crowd ourselves ever more densely into our cities, we can expect increases in mental illness, sexual dysfunction, fetal mortality, infant mortality, heart disease, crime, violence, juvenile delinquency, poor health, and social disorganization simply because we have activated our species' survival mechanisms? As we shall see, some social scientists think this is the case, while others are not convinced. The outcome of this debate, however, is more than academic because it has important implications for the types of urban and population policies our society should adopt.

MEANWHILE IN THE CITY

While it is possible that something analogous (or even identical) to the species survival mechanisms of animals exists in humans, it is a great inferential leap from the animal research simply to assume that it does exist. In the first place, the behavioral and physiological reactions of animals to extreme crowding are species-specific. That is, when crowded, some animals exhibit some of the behaviors of Calhoun's rats, other animals exhibit others, while still others exhibit an entirely different set of behaviors. Similarly, the specific physiological reactions documented by Christian will vary from species to species, although these reactions appear to be centered in one part or other of the endocrine system. Thus, we cannot be certain whether humans will exhibit all or any of the behaviors of the rats in Calhoun's study.

More important, humans have more ability to think symbolically than any other animal. This means that humans can both look into the future and create culture. Either of these abilities could serve the same evolutionary functions as the physiological reactions and (apparently) instinctive behaviors of animals. Hence, these more primitive mechanisms may have been bred out of human beings long ago. Consistent with this point of view is Deevey's (1960) work, which suggests that people have always used some means of voluntary birth control to maintain a constant population level until a major technical or cultural breakthrough permitted a larger population to be supported by the increased food supply. Deevey hypothesized that these breakthroughs probably occurred between 100,000 and a million years ago when toolmaking and culture developed, between 6,000 and 10,000 years ago following the agricultural revolution, and about 300 years ago when the scientific-industrial revolution began. Over this million-year span, the population of the world grew from around 10,000 to about 10 billion persons.

It is clear, then, that we must follow the advice of Calhoun and Christian and be very cautious in generalizing from animal studies to people. We need to examine closely studies of the effects of density and crowding upon humans. Social psychologists have only recently begun studies of this sort, but a few sociologists, economists, and demographers have been doing studies of population density and crowding in human aggregates for some time. What do these studies reveal?

The first systematic research in this area was based on 1950 census data for the city of Honolulu and was done by Robert C. Schmitt. Schmitt's first study (1957) examined the correlations of (1) population density (as measured by number of people per acre), (2) average household size, (3) married couples without their own households, (4) dwelling units in structures with five or more units, and (5) occupied dwelling units with 1.51 or more persons per room with two measures of social pathology—crime and juvenile delinquency rates. He found that of these five measures of population density, only two (gross density and number of persons per room) were consistently related to both crime and delinquency. For example, in census tracts with under twenty persons per acre, the crime rate was .66 (number of adult offenders per 1,000 adults) and the delinquency rate was 15.8 (number of juvenile offenders per 1,000 families) while in tracts having sixty or more persons per acre, the crime and delinquency rates were 1.72 and 25.5, respectively. That is, as gross population density and number of persons per room increased so did the measures of social pathology.

Schmitt's second study (1966), which also used 1950 Honolulu census data, was considerably more sophisticated. In it he looked at the individual and combined correlations of the five density variables of the first study with death rate, infant death rate, suicide rate, tuberculosis rate, venereal disease rate, mental hospital admission rate, illegitimate birth rate, juvenile delinquency rate, and prison admission rate. He found that the relationships between his density measures and these nine measures of health and social disorganization were very strong. The multiple correlations (which take into account the *joint* effect of all input variables) between his density measures and the nine hypothesized effects ranged from .859 (for venereal disease rate) to .409 (for infant mortality) with a median of .771 (for tuberculosis rate). High population density, therefore, went hand in hand with poor health and heightened social disorganization. Furthermore, after applying a technique known as partial correlation (which identifies the *unique* contribution of each individual input variable) he concluded that gross density was the best predictor of his nine health and disorganization measures.

A study made about the same time by Winsborough (1965) produced similar results. Using 1950 Chicago census data, Winsborough found that population density was related to an increase in death rate, infant mortality, tuberculosis rate, and public assistance (or welfare) rate. In addition, Seiver (1971), using 1960 census data, found a significant (though small) correlation between population density and white fetal mortality in New York State and across the twenty-one largest cities of the United States. Thus, if we stopped here, we might conclude that both mice and men react to density in the same general ways: they become more aggressive, their infants and adults die or become sick, and their social structures and institutions disintegrate. But, alas, the world of humans is more complex than we have pictured it so far.

The first complication we must consider is social class. Frequently the poor and less educated live in the crowded central cores of our cities, where we find the most crime and delinquency, the poorest health and health care (see Chapter 3), and the greatest degree of social disorganization (as defined by middle-class social scientists). On the other hand, the more affluent metropolitan dwellers generally live in the suburbs, where crime, delinquency, poor health, and social disorganization are relatively less likely to occur. Therefore, it is entirely possible that density and social pathology are not directly related at all but are both symptoms of being poor or uneducated.

In Schmitt's first study (1957), he made no attempt to control for education and income; he did so in his second study (1966), and found that the density correlation still remained significant (though somewhat reduced). However, as Freedman et al. (1971) have pointed out, his controls for education and income were such as to minimize their effect and hence, his remaining relationships between density and pathology are highly suspect.[2] Furthermore, when other researchers applied controls for education and income, they found that the correlations between density and social pathology were either reduced to an unsubstantial, though still significant, level (Seiver, 1971) or that they were reversed for the most part (Winsborough, 1965). That is, after applying controls for social class, Winsborough found that a high death rate, tuberculosis rate, and public assistance rate were associated with *less* density rather than more. Finally, in the most sophisticated aggregate study to date, Galle et al. (1972) found that all the density relationships with their dependent measures (see below) could be accounted for by social class and ethnicity. It appears, then, that mice and men are not affected by density in the same way.

Alternatively, population density may not be the factor affecting mice (or rats), either. In both Calhoun's and Christian's studies, the land area or space remained constant, while the number of animals

_____

[2]This critique is on a very sophisticated methodological level. For those who are interested it can be found in Freedman et al. (1971).

increased. This means that both density (number of animals per acre or square foot) *and* total number of animals increased. Though most social scientists have interpreted the effects as resulting from the increased density (cf. the title of Calhoun's paper: "Population Density and Social Pathology"), it is possible that they resulted from the necessity of having to deal and interact with so many creatures of the same species.

The problem becomes even more complex as we move from animal studies to research with humans, because people have the technology to create very dense populations (number of persons per unit of land area) with a minimum of crowding (number of persons per room).[3] Thus, in the animal realm, density and crowding (except in a few species) are almost synonymous, but in humans they are quite distinct. For example, it is possible to have high crowding in a situation of very low density as when six members of a tenant farmer's family live in a one-room shack which is the only dwelling in a two-square-mile area. Conversely, we can have high density but relatively little crowding in high-rise luxury apartments.

Carey (1972) suggests that as nations become increasingly technologically and economically developed, the empirical relationship, or correlation, between density and crowding in urban areas will decline almost to zero. In America this relationship is already low: .270 for Washington, D.C., .276 for Manhattan (Carey, 1972) and .146 in Chicago[4] (Galle et al., 1972). Therefore, it is entirely possible that, in addition to the total number of persons or social interactions, crowding itself might adversely affect people.

Studies on the total number of interactions have yet to be done, but one very careful and sophisticated aggregate study of humans lends

[3] One psychologist, Daniel Stokols (1972), would distinguish density from crowding in another fashion. He has suggested that the term *density* should be reserved for descriptions of external, spatial factors while the term *crowding* should be used only to describe the internal perceptual and motivational states resulting from the interaction of spatial and personal factors. In his schema, both of our terms would be subsumed under the term density since both number of persons per unit of land area and number of persons per room are external spatial factors. We chose to use the terms as we did because this parallels their usage in the older sociological and demographic literature (Carey, 1972; Galle et al., 1972) and because psychologists have yet to develop fully adequate measures of the internal state of crowding hypothesized by Stokols.

[4] All these coefficients were computed using 1960 census data.

a great deal of support to the crowding (as opposed to the density) hypothesis. Using 1960 census data for Chicago, three sociologists at Vanderbilt University, Omer R. Galle, Walter R. Gove, and J. Miller McPherson, examined (1) density, (2) crowding, (3) rooms per housing unit, (4) housing units per structure, and (5) structures per acre as predictors of four social pathologies: (1) mortality ratio, (2) general fertility rate, (3) juvenile delinquency rate, and (4) admission to mental hospitals.[5] As reported above, simple density was uncorrelated with the four pathologies when ethnicity (race) and social class were controlled. However, a combined measure of the other components of density showed a fairly high correlation with the pathologies after controls for social class and ethnicity were applied. Most important, for three of the four pathologies, crowding (number of persons per room) was the most powerful predictor of the effect.[6]

The results of this study lend strong support to the idea that social class and ethnicity affect mortality ratio, fertility rate, etc. both directly (see Chapter 3) and by mediation through crowding, which also has an independent effect upon the pathologies. That is, over and above any effect produced directly by social class and ethnicity, there is an effect produced by crowding.

How do these pathologies associated with crowding in Chicago compare with the behaviors noted in Calhoun's rats? The mortality ratio is directly comparable to the death rate among the rats; as crowding increased so did mortality. Juvenile delinquency among human males may be roughly parallel to the aggressiveness of male rats, and crowding and delinquency were positively related. However, general fertility rate requires some translating and interpreting to fit Calhoun's findings.

[5] Galle and his associates also analyzed the correlations between their density and crowding variables and a fifth pathology: the number of recipients of public assistance under eighteen years old. We omit discussion of it here because we think it was a very poor indicator of "ineffectual parental care of the young," the behavior of Calhoun's rats that it was supposed to reflect. Unless one wishes to blame the victim (Ryan, 1971), it could be argued that the public assistance rate is a measure of parental concern rather than ineffectualness. We hasten to to add that Galle et al. were themselves uneasy about this measure.

[6] For admission to mental hospitals, the most powerful correlate was rooms per housing unit, another possible measure of crowding or lack of privacy for humans.

In the animal studies, the birth rates dropped drastically due to miscarriages. The decline in fertility, combined with increases in infant mortality and the adult death rate, reduced the population in a very short time. Yet, Galle et al. (1972) found that general fertility—the number of births in an area per 1,000 women between fifteen and forty-four years old—increased as crowding increased. While crowding hardly appears to be a mechanism for population control, we can well understand how greater proximity might lead to increased fertility. It may be, as Galle and his associates suggest, that the increase in the fertility rate is a reflection of one of Calhoun's other findings: that crowding produced hypersexuality. This hypothesis cannot be tested, however, with any existing aggregate data.

THE PROBLEMS OF AGGREGATION AND CORRELATION

Many, if not most, social psychologists would be quite uneasy with the findings of these aggregate correlational studies of density and crowding in humans. First of all, the analyses are based upon aggregate- rather than individual-level data. By aggregate data we mean the characteristics of two or more persons grouped together, or aggregated, for purposes of analysis. The persons in the aggregates may be to some extent aware that they have been grouped as, for example, when the units of analysis are family units, cities, states, or countries. On the other hand, the persons concerned may have little idea that they are members of the specific group that the researcher is interested in, as when the units of analysis are census tracts, health districts, or units of uniform area imposed upon a map of a city by a demographer. Psychologists, because of their concern with the behavior of individuals, usually do individual-level studies rather than aggregate-level ones. The difference between the two types is that aggregate analysis is concerned with the relationship between characteristics of the aggregate (e.g., percentage black and percentage voting Democrat in a voting precinct) while individual-level analysis is concerned with the relationship between characteristics of individuals (e.g., race of person and tendency of that same person to vote Democrat).

Aggregate data, then, have two weaknesses for those concerned with the feelings and behaviors of individuals. First, it is logically impossible to generalize from studies based upon the behavior of aggregates (cities, states, census tracts) to the behavior of individual people having characteristics similar to those of the aggregates. Second, while aggregate and individual analyses often lead to the same conclusion, there are times when they do not. For example, the aggregate correlation between percent foreign-born and percent illiterate in one study was -.62 while at the individual level the correlation between being foreign born and illiterate was +.12! In another study, the correlation between percent black and percent illiterate in a census tract was +.95 while at the individual level the correlation was only +.20 (Shively, 1969). In both examples the differences were so great that any individual-level conclusions drawn on the basis of the aggregate analysis would have been completely wrong or seriously misleading.

In addition to being based upon aggregate data, the studies are also correlational in nature, another difficulty from the standpoint of psychologists who are trained for the most part in an experimental approach to research questions. In correlational studies, it is impossible to make an unambiguous inference about the direction of causation. For example, persons who are in poor health, or about to die, may wish to be in closer proximity to other people than those who are in good health.[7] Thus, poor health and high death rates may be the cause of crowding rather than the reverse, as has been assumed. In addition, the statistical controls for socioeconomic status (e.g., social class and ethnicity) are mathematical approximations at best, and may be either inadequate or too sensitive.[8] In addition, while socioeconomic status is the factor most likely to account for both crowding and the various pathological behaviors, there just might be another set of factors (as yet to be discovered) that caused all three: socioeconomic status, crowding, and pathology.

[7]This assertion is not as wild as it might seem at first glance; cf. Schachter's (1959) work on fear and affiliation.

[8]For specific criticisms of the controls in Schmitt's (1957, 1966) and Winsborough's (1965) studies, see Freedman et al. (1971). For a general discussion of the problems of mathematical controls in correlational research, see McConahay (1973).

RESULTS FROM THE LABORATORY

An experimental approach which uses random assignment[9] to equate the groups of persons and to control for extraneous factors can overcome all these objections. Therefore, we shall look closely at the results of the few experimental studies done by social psychologists.

The most extensive series of experimental studies of crowding was conducted by Jonathan L. Freedman and his associates (Freedman, 1971, Freedman et al., 1971; Freedman et al., 1972). In their studies, groups of either five or nine persons were put in rooms of 160, 80, and 35 square feet for periods of up to four hours. The same groups of five or nine people worked in each of the three rooms on successive days. The investigators reasoned (before the experiments began) that the groups of nine subjects would be relatively crowded in the small and middle-sized rooms and relatively uncrowded in the large room, and that the groups of five subjects would be relatively crowded only in the small room and relatively uncrowded in the middle-sized and large rooms. All the rooms were well ventilated, air-conditioned, acoustically comfortable, and nicely appointed so that such factors as odor, lack of oxygen, heat, humidity, noise, and physical discomfort were held constant across experimental conditions. Most important, since a person was always in the same group of either five or nine subjects, density and crowding varied as the groups moved from room to room, but the number of persons did not. Thus, in these studies as in the Calhoun studies, crowding and density were identical. But unlike the Calhoun studies, these did *not* confound density with the number of subjects or the number of potential social interactions.

After a twenty-minute discussion of a current problem such as what might be done to reduce highway accidents, the groups of subjects worked on a series of mental tasks, took a short break, and then resumed the same series of tasks using new materials. In subsequent studies, the subjects worked at experimental games in which they could be either competitive or cooperative, discussed criminal cases and

---

[9] By random assignment, we mean a procedure which makes any given individual as likely to be put in a crowded as in an uncrowded condition. For an elementary discussion of the techniques and benefits of random assignment, see McConahay (1973).

sentenced the offenders, and indicated how much they liked other members of the group.

The investigators found that thinking and reasoning were not affected by crowding. Persons could work as well on simple and complex reasoning problems in both crowded and uncrowded conditions (Freedman et al., 1971). On the other hand, social behavior was somewhat altered by the change from crowded to uncrowded conditions (Freedman, 1971). As crowding increased, males became more competitive, more severe in the sentences they meted out to criminals, and liked their cohorts less *when*, and this is very important, they were in *all-male* groups. However, as crowding increased, females reacted in the opposite way. In *all-female* groups they became less competitive (more cooperative), less severe in their sentencing, and liked their cohorts more. When *males and females* were in the *same group*, crowding had no effect upon either the behavior of the entire group or upon men and women separately.

To summarize: Freedman's research found that work upon cognitive (thinking and reasoning) tasks was not impaired by short-term (four hours maximum) crowding and neither were interpersonal liking, competition, or aggression when the persons worked in groups composed of both males and females. When the subjects worked in groups composed of all males or all females, as crowding increased, the males became more competitive, more aggressive, and liked their cohorts less while the females reacted in the opposite fashion.

Another published experimental study of crowding yielded somewhat different results. Griffitt and Veitch (1971) created a crowded (high-density) and uncrowded (low-density) condition by working with all-male or all-female groups of three to five or twelve to sixteen subjects in the same room. They found that *both* men and women subjects were less likely to be attracted to a hypothetical other person as the crowding increased. They did not find a significant effect of crowding upon aggressiveness in either sex. However, these results are not directly comparable to those of Freedman et al., because Griffitt and Veitch did not distinguish between density and the number of persons interacting. Thus, the different findings of the two studies might be the result of this lack of distinction in the second study.

WHERE DO WE STAND (OR SIT) THEN?

So what can we conclude about the existing research into the effects of crowding upon humans? First, and most obviously, we need a great deal more research. Few of the findings, except Freedman's (1971), have been replicated using different subject populations. And while some of the experimental studies have been able to look at crowding or density independently of the total number of experienced (or anticipated) social interactions and some of the aggregate studies have been able to separate the effects of crowding from those of density, none has been able to examine all three factors (crowding, density, and number of persons or interactions) independently. In addition, while the correlational studies dealt with long-term or chronic crowding, the laboratory studies dealt only with short-term or acute crowding (in an atmosphere which limited the physical discomforts of crowding). It may be that crowding effects emerge only in chronic situations or that persons from backgrounds of long-term crowding will react differently to acute crowding situations. Finally, none of the studies so far has explored the factor of perceived privacy. It may be that people can endure great density and crowding, and numerous interactions if they feel they can have privacy whenever they want to get away from it all.

Second, what we conclude from the existing research depends upon the questions asked. We asked: To what extent does population density per se trigger some innate population-control mechanism in humans? In answering this question we give the most weight to the aggregate study of Galle et al. (1972) and the experimental work of Freedman et al. (1972), because we think these are the best of the existing published studies.[10]

Our answer to the question, then, is that we have not seen much evidence that population density per se triggers any innate mechanisms for population control. It may be that crowding and/or the total number of people do trigger innate mechanisms leading to violence, aggres-

---

[10]We already indicated why we thought the Galle et al. study was the best of the aggregate studies. We think the Freedman et al. work should have the most weight among the experimental studies because it was the most extensive, had the widest range of subjects (all were American, but they ranged in age from seventeen to ninety and covered most of the ethnic spectrum in America where-as Griffitt and Veitch studied only college students) and employed experimental designs that were less likely to inform the subjects of their intentions in the study. See McConahay (1973) for discussions of demand characteristics in experimental designs.

sion, hypersexuality, sexual "deviance," high adult mortality, infant and fetal mortality, and mental illness, but the case either for their innateness or their inevitability is not yet proven. The work of Galle et al. suggests that crowding and factors which may accompany crowding are correlated with some population limiting factors, but the work of Galle et al. suggests that the population-limiting behaviors of aggression and hostility need not emerge inevitably from (short-term) density or crowding per se. In fact, Freedman's findings are consistent with the hypothesis that the higher mental processes of complex reasoning and thinking as well as the primitive reactions of aggression and hostility are unaffected by density per se. If this is true, our cities' problems are not the result of having too many people, but of what all those people are doing and bringing with them. We shall examine the implications of this for social policy in the last section of this chapter.

THE ODOR AND THE CLANGOR

Though there is scant evidence that population density in and of itself produces unpleasant behavior changes in people that might lead to drastic limitations on population growth, we do not think that people crowd together into cities without incurring some cost. In small towns people make a certain amount of noise, pour a few hydrocarbons and carbon dioxide into the air, and dump their waste into the water. In large towns and cities, the crowds make a terrible clamor, make the air unfit to breathe, and cause the water to be unfit to drink. Those who do not leave the cities for rural areas must either attack the problems of noise, air, and water pollution directly in order to get them reduced to tolerable levels or they must adjust to them. In most cases they adjust. Psychologists have only recently begun to examine the psychic costs of adjustment to noise pollution, while the effects of air and water pollution have not been studied at all.

The popular press has not, however, been reluctant to speculate about the effects of air and noise pollution. In the hours immediately following the onset of the Los Angeles riots, *The New York Times* expressed the opinion that the heat and smog of mid-August were responsible (Sears & McConahay, 1973). As we indicate in Chapter 6, we think political and social psychological factors were much more important in producing the rioting than were heat or smog, but Griffitt and Veitch (1971) found that aggressive responses increased with increasing heat. Hence, heat (and smog) may make people significantly more hostile or aggressive, and could raise the level of annoyance of people who were already annoyed and angry to a critical point where a small, otherwise insignificant, incident could set off a violent outburst. Such an outburst might take the form of murder, suicide, rioting, or revolution.

In the realm of noise pollution we have more data to guide us, although much more work still needs to be done. In a highly coordinated series of experimental studies, David C. Glass and Jerome E. Singer (1972) demonstrated that noise can affect certain behaviors and that, although people can adjust to noise, they pay a psychic price for their adjustment.

These investigators found that, when working on most tasks, subjects (young and old, male and female, college students and non-college students) who were exposed to a sequence of high-intensity sounds (108 dBA) over a twenty-five- to thirty-minute period performed as well as similar subjects who had not been exposed to the sounds. However, when the tasks were complex and demanded a great deal of information processing, and when the noise was perceived by the subjects as unpredictable and uncontrollable, performance decreased markedly.

As we indicated above, in most adverse circumstances, people adapt to the situation rather than leave it or take steps to change it. The subjects of Glass and Singer's experiments, like most urban dwellers, adapted to the noise. After a while, the subjects in the most extreme noise-stress conditions working on the most complex tasks reduced their number of errors and their physiological reactions virtually to the level of that of subjects not exposed to noise stress. Yet, after the noise was removed, the persons who had been under this stress performed more poorly on cognitive tasks, showed less tolerance of frustration, and had less ability to resolve conflicts than those who had not been under the stress. The persons under stress had adjusted to the unpredictable and uncontrollable noise, but they had paid a price that was reflected in subsequent behavior in conditions without stress.

Similar findings emerged from a study of sleep disruption by noise (Roth et al., 1971). Persons who had their sleep disrupted at crucial periods were not affected by this in their performance of simple tasks the next day, but were definitely impaired in their performance of complex cognitive tasks involving memory, mathematical reasoning, and time estimation. Furthermore, the older the age group, the more the noise-disrupted sleep impaired complex daytime functioning.

Thus, the denizens of our cities who are bombarded with the unpredictable and uncontrollable high-intensity noise of freeways, subways, jet airports, jackhammers, neighbors' stereos, school playgrounds and countless other noise generators suffer from a very effective "one-two punch." The noise we adapt to at work will make us irritable and unable to do complex cognitive tasks at home (such as balancing the family bankbook or keeping appropriate tax records) and the noise which disrupts our sleep will make us irritable and unable to function on complex tasks at work. Of course, a social class bias operates in determining who suffers from noise pollution. Jet landing corridors and the land immediately adjacent to freeways, to cite two of many possible examples, are either selected by the city and federal government for that purpose because poor and/or minorities already live in the areas or else such areas soon become populated with poor and minority groups because no one else wants to live there. Nevertheless, all city dwellers are exposed to some noise pollution during the course of the day. Those at the bottom of the socioeconomic ladder pay the highest psychic price, but everyone pays something for living close to so many other people.

ADAPTATIONS TO SOCIAL OVERLOAD

All those people not only fill our cities with air and noise pollution; they also increase the number of potential social interactions we must endure each day. As we indicated in our discussion of population density and crowding, we have little hard data regarding the effects of too many potential social interactions upon the population control mechanisms of animals and humans. We do, however, have some very perceptive speculations by social psychologist Stanley Milgram about the effects of too many potential interactions upon other types of human urban behavior.

The basic starting point of Milgram's (1970) analysis is the concept of overload, which in systems analysis refers to a system's inability to process inputs from the environment either because there are too many inputs or because the inputs come so fast that the system cannot cope with them. City life, he suggests, threatens us with continuous sets of social encounters (i.e., "interpersonal overload") and we adapt to them much as a computer or other system does. How does this happen?

First, we allocate less time to each input. Second, we disregard low-priority inputs by adoption of explicit or implicit principles of selectivity as when we disregard the antics or sufferings of strangers while making our way through a subway crowd. Third, we redraw the boundaries in certain social transactions as when bus drivers and some store owners shift the responsibility for making change from themselves to the rider or customer. Fourth, we block off reception prior to its entry into our system as when we get unlisted phone numbers or simply leave the phone off the hook. Fifth, we interpose filtering devices between ourselves and the inputs so that the intensity of the inputs is diminished. This is usually expressed as an unwillingness to get involved in the lives of more than just a few people. For example, Tucker and Friedman (1972) found that students at a large university ate in smaller groups and in fewer bisexual groups than students at a smaller university. Sixth, and finally, we demand and create specialized institutions such as welfare agencies to absorb inputs that might otherwise swamp the individual. As a result of these adaptations to overload (or potential overload) life in our cities is marked by diminished individual social responsibility in times of crisis and increased superficiality, anonymity, and transitoriness in personal relations.

SO WHAT CAN WE DO?

Before tackling the question of what we could possibly do about the problems of too much in our cities, we will briefly summarize what little is known about the psychological aspects of these problems.

First, we know very little because very little systematic research has been conducted up to this time. This must be stressed because it emphasizes the tentativeness of our other conclusions.

Second, population density (number of persons per unit of land area) per se *does not* appear to trigger in humans the severe population-limiting behaviors that emerged in animal studies: violence, aggression, competition for space, hypersexuality, sexual "deviance," high adult mortality (possibly due to endocrine system malfunction), high infant mortality, high fetal mortality, and mental illness. The best of both the aggregate studies and the laboratory studies support this conclusion. On the other hand, the aggregate study of Galle et al. (1972) did find that crowding (number of persons per room) was associated with higher death, fertility, and juvenile delinquency rates while the number of rooms per housing unit, another possible measure of crowding or lack of privacy, was positively related to admissions to mental hospitals. Comparable results did not emerge in the short-term laboratory crowding studies, however, and the results can be explained for humans without resorting to hypothesized "innate" or biological population-control mechanisms.

Third, the by-products of density and crowding (noise, definitely, and air pollution, possibly)[11] do result in annoyance and interfere with work on complex tasks, although people can certainly adjust to even the most severe conditions (i.e., when the noise is unpredictable and uncontrollable).

Fourth, people can adjust to noise and social overload, but they pay a price. In the case of noise, Glass and Singer (1972) found that the price is irritability and poor performance on subsequent complex tasks. In the case of social overload, Milgram (1970) has suggested that the price is reduced individual social responsibility and increased superficiality, anonymity, and transitoriness in personal relations.

Finally, we would suggest that a strong theme running through these data and speculations is perceived personal control. Glass and Singer demonstrated that the cost of adjustment to noise is lower when the individual perceives that he or she can control it, and Milgram's analysis suggests that the diminished social responsibility, and so on, of the urban dwellers resulted from attempts to exert control over social overload. We suspect that the possibility of privacy or escape provided

----

[11] In calling noise and air pollution the by-products of density and crowding we are well aware that they are also the by-products of industrialization and technological development. If unchecked or unregulated, these technological by-products will pollute the whole world and exhaust its resources. However, the immediate problems of noise and air pollution are most critical in the cities, where more people crowded together means more concentrated noise and gaseous, liquid, and solid chemical wastes to be dealt with.

by uncrowded quarters even in very densely populated locales is what accounts for differential effects of crowding and density upon people.

So what do these findings imply for what we might do? We cannot answer that question in detail but we can suggest some approaches.

First, the by-products of crowding (noise and air pollution) are subject to some degree to technological solution. Our cities could be made less noisy through the use of proper acoustics in our construction and through less noise emission by our machines. Similarly, more efficient, less polluting sources of energy could be developed and utilized so that our cars, homes, and factories do not foul the air and water. These technological solutions will not occur, however, so long as it is profitable for individuals and industries to create noise and air pollution. That means we must raise both the psychological costs (by informal social norms) and the legal and economic costs of pollution by passing ordinances, building codes, zoning laws, licensing laws, and taxation laws that make it too expensive to pollute.

Second, the (tentative) discovery that we can live in conditions of fairly high population density without killing ourselves so long as we are not overly crowded in our dwelling (or life) space raises the possibility of a partial technical solution in this area also. We could, *if it became necessary*, stack roomy and nonpolluting housing units on top of one another to conserve land space. This would allow us to devote more land to food production and protect our scenic wonders from residential development in order to give people the option of having privacy in the city or that of getting away from the city for brief respites from social overload (see Ward et al., 1972, for a discussion of how privacy and protection from social overload could be built into dwelling units). Again, this partial technological solution will not be developed unless we create the appropriate social, economic, and legal conditions. (How psychology can contribute to this process is discussed in Chapter 8.)

However, both these technical solutions are only partial and short-term answers to the cities' current problems of too much. Our nation's and our planet's space and resources are finite. If population growth and resource consumption continue unchecked, all the world will have the same problems as our cities. Hence, any long-term solution must involve a stable, nonexpanding population both in this country and around the world. That is, we will have to use our abilities to look into the future as a substitute for the population control mechanisms of animals.

Third, the importance of perceptions of control over urban stresses suggests that we will have to develop social and political institutions that will permit individuals to control those aspects of the urban environment over which they have no control at present (except in the case of the very rich or those who can exercise the option of leaving the entire scene). For example, while some people thoroughly enjoy the stimulation provided by amplified rock music, others do not. At present much of our cities' social and physical environment is such that the two preferences must be treated as incompatible. If rock fans get their wish, the other people cannot have theirs. The proper structuring of these environments will test our ingenuity, but this must be attempted.

Finally, our administrative and legislative structures must be made more responsive to the people they serve. As we shall see in subsequent chapters, this will be very difficult to achieve because there are real differences in values and interests among the various segments of our pluralistic culture. At present, though, our legislatures and bureaucracies respond mainly to the interests of the white middle class or to those of the people who staff the bureaucracies (usually drawn from the white middle class; cf. Chapters 4 and 6). Glass and Singer (1972) have suggested the need for an urban ombudsman to look after the interests of the individual who is fighting the government bureaucracy. We think this would be an important start.

Chapter 3

The Problems of Too Little

In the early and middle 1960s a number of divergent forces came together to bring the problem of poverty into the awareness of a large number of Americans. Those who experienced firsthand the problems of too little—too little work, too little income, too little food, too little medical care—needed no reminder that poverty is a reality even in the United States, the world's richest nation. The public at large, however, did need reminding. The civil rights movement did much to highlight the plight of the Southern black; the urban riots made Americans forcefully aware of poverty in inner-city ghettos. Michael Harrington's (1962) book *The Other America* brought the fact of poverty to a wide audience, and poverty became a significant national issue when Lyndon Johnson called for a "national war on poverty" in 1964.

In the period since these events, social scientists have devoted much effort to understanding the problems of too little, with an emphasis on attempting to come up with and evaluate proposals for alleviating these problems. This chapter will cover those efforts. Although poor people can be found in all parts of America, poverty—and the related questions of unemployment and substandard housing—is increasingly becoming an urban problem.[1] As we saw in Chapter 1, the migration of Southern rural blacks to the cities during the last fifty years is one of the biggest population shifts experienced by our nation. People left their homes in hopes of finding jobs and a better existence in the cities. Some were able to accomplish this goal; many others, however, found their lot was just as uncertain in the urban centers to which they moved. As our nation continues to become more urbanized—with whites, Puerto Ricans, and others joining in the movement to metropolitan areas—poverty becomes increasingly a part of the syndrome of urban problems. Consequently, the research we will cover is concerned primarily, although not exclusively, with urban poverty. Although much of what we will say is relevant to rural poverty, not all of it can be directly transposed from the urban to the nonurban setting.

During the 1960s American behavioral scientists (anthropologists, political scientists, sociologists, and psychologists) attempted to develop theories to explain poverty at the level of the individual poor person and his immediate community. Two major schools of thought developed—one is popularly known as the *culture of poverty* while the second we will call *structural determinism.* These schools of thought are not mutually exclusive; they simply stress different factors as important in understanding poverty. As we shall see, both approaches offer insight into this multifaceted problem. We begin with the culture-of-poverty explanation because it is the more widely known and it has had greater impact on recent federal antipoverty efforts (Gladwin, 1967 p. 26).

The culture-of-poverty concept was developed and most fully articulated by the anthropologist Oscar Lewis (1959, 1966, 1968). According to Lewis, under certain conditions people living in poverty (". . . the absence of something," usually economic resources) develop their own subculture, which tends to perpetuate itself, as well as the attendant poverty, through time. A culture is "a way of life that is passed down from generation to generation along family lines" (Lewis, 1968, p.187). Although anthropologists often disagree about what exactly is meant by the phrase "a way of life" it is enough for our purposes to think of this as including such things as attitudes, values, personality traits, food

---

[1] The extent and nature of rural poverty are well documented in a report entitled *The People Left Behind* (1967).

habits, language, and religion. Lewis feels that the culture of poverty represents a combination "of some seventy interrelated social, economic, and psychological traits."

Although the culture of poverty can develop in almost any historical or societal setting, it is most likely to occur in modern capitalist nation-states, especially during periods of rapid technological change. As this description fits the present-day United States, it is easy to see how people could interpret Lewis as talking about the blacks and other minorities inhabiting our central cities. Lewis himself, however, is not too clear on this point: at times he uses the culture-of-poverty concept to explain "Negro family life in the United States" (1968, p.198), but at another point he specifically says that only about 20 percent of those officially defined as "poor" in the United States would he describe as living in the culture of poverty (1968, p.196). Thus, Lewis seems to be talking about only that extreme group of the poor among whom poverty has become a way of life. Since others have used the culture-of-poverty concept to describe the situation of our urban ghettos (e.g., Harrington, 1962, p.16), it would be desirable to elucidate this concept further and to see if the available evidence supports its application to the American urban poor as a group.

Lewis sees the culture of poverty as an adaptation to the fact of being poor. Being poor means having no job or low-paying inconsistent employment, inferior housing, no savings. This state of affairs in turn produces the traits of the culture of poverty. Those living in the culture of poverty do not, for example, participate in the major institutions of the larger society; that is, they don't vote, belong to the PTA, and so on. At the local level there is little community organization (i.e., clubs, special interest groups, fraternal organizations) beyond the family. In terms of family life there is a high incidence of broken marriages, mother-centered families, and harsh, punitive child-rearing practices. And, finally, the culture of poverty entails a number of psychological traits, among the most important being feelings of helplessness and inferiority, "lack of impulse control, strong present-time orientation . . . [and a] sense of resignation and fatalism" (Lewis, 1968, p. 192). In sum, the culture of poverty is a set of individual and community devices for coping with economic deprivation.

Lewis' major point, then, is that the culture of poverty is self-perpetuating because children reared in these circumstances adopt the

basic values, attitudes, and behaviors of their subculture by the time
they reach the age of seven or eight. These values, attitudes, and
behaviors place psychological limitations upon the youngsters' abilities
to take advantage of most opportunities for escaping the culture of
poverty and changing their lives (Lewis, 1968, p.188). This position
has important implications for social policy: if poor people are seen
as having a culture that perpetuates poverty and that makes it difficult
or impossible for them to take advantage of economic and social
opportunity, then efforts to eradicate poverty simply by altering
economic conditions will not work. For example, if Lewis is right,
providing poor people with good jobs and adequate housing will not
work because their culture has not prepared them to take advantage of
those opportunities. The sense of helplessness, apathy, and present-
time orientation would interfere with adequate job performance. Lewis'
position suggests that *both* economic conditions *and* some aspects of
culture must be changed if poverty is to be eliminated. The stress,
however, is on culture change. We will return to policy considerations
later in the chapter; for the moment we direct our attention to evaluating the culture-of-poverty formulation.

EVALUATION OF THE CULTURE OF POVERTY

A number of social scientists have criticized the culture-of-poverty
concept, especially when used to explain the behavior of America's
urban poor (Allen, 1970; Gans, 1968; Liebow, 1967; Rainwater, 1968;
Rossi & Blum, 1968; Valentine, 1968). Here we will attempt to
summarize and organize these criticisms. Most objections fall into
one of three general categories: (1) the logic of the culture of poverty
as a theory; (2) the *data* relevant to the theory; and (3) the *implications*
of the theory.

Problems with the Logic of the Culture-of-Poverty Theory

Although not completely explicit in the writings of Lewis and others,
the culture-of-poverty position implies that the poor are *qualitatively*
different from the nonpoor; there is a difference in kind, not in amount,
between the poor and nonpoor with regard to certain traits. A compre-

hensive review of the empirical evidence on these traits, however, revealed that

> ...in almost every case it is clear that the alleged "special" characteristics of the poor are ones that they share generally with the "working-class" or "blue-collar" component of the labor force. In other words, the poor *are* different, but the difference appears mainly to be a matter of *degree* rather than of kind (Rossi & Blum, 1968, p.39).

Related to this is the fact that many traits ascribed to the culture of poverty are also part of mainstream American culture. For example, Valentine (1968) points out that "male dominance," which is often attributed to the culture of poverty, is certainly not exclusive to it. In other words, the urban poor are not so distinctively different or "special" as the culture-of-poverty idea suggests.

A much more significant criticism of the logic of the culture-of-poverty formulation is that it confuses what people do with what they want. Gans (1968) notes that there is often a divergence between what people aspire to (*aspirations*) and what they allow themselves and others to do (*behavioral norms*). If one looks simply at what happens in many ghetto neighborhoods one might conclude that marriage as an institution is devalued (because there is a high incidence of premarital sex and many married couples are separated), crime is highly valued (because the crime rate tends to be high in inner-city areas), and cleanliness is not felt to be important (because the people are often ill-dressed and the neighborhoods decaying). All three of these conclusions, however, would be wrong. In a questionnaire study of poor families living in an urban public housing project, it was found that most people felt that "lifelong marriage is the only really desirable way of living..." (Rainwater, 1968, p. 237). And, rather than valuing crime, poor people fear it. In a poll of New Jersey adults, blacks, who live primarily in in inner-city ghettos, listed "crime" as the number one problem confronting their state. (Whites felt that property taxes were the state's biggest problem.) And Sternlieb and Indik (1973) found that fear of crime was the primary reason tenants were moving out of a New York City public housing project. Finally, does the filthiness of the ghetto mean that ghetto residents don't value cleanliness? Rokeach and

Parker (1970) found that the value of cleanliness was the single biggest difference between a national sample of poor and nonpoor Americans: the poor felt it was *very* important, the nonpoor, relatively unimportant. (This does not mean that the more affluent are indifferent to cleanliness, only that their position in life does not make cleanliness a salient concern.)

In summary, there are often radical differences between what the poor aspire to and how they actually behave.[2] How do these disjunctures come about? First, the poor as well as the affluent aspire to many aspects of mainstream culture (a good job, a comfortable house, a happy family) because they are exposed to it via the mass media and the educational system. Second, the realities of economic deprivation plus discrimination make the attainment of many mainstream goals impossible. For example, lack of income leads to conflicts between husband and wife over spending their limited resources and this conflict spreads into other areas of the marriage, thus making it less viable. In addition, our welfare laws make support more available to *single* women with children, thus reducing pressures "to stay together for the kids' sake." Therefore, even though stable marriages are valued by those in lower socioeconomic strata, the realities of being poor often make the attainment of the value impossible.

Discrepancies in the Data Regarding the Culture-of-Poverty Formulation

The first thing apparent to reviewers of empirical research on the poor is that there isn't very much of it and what there is is often not very conclusive. In a subsequent section we will cover variables that *do* characterize the poor. Our point here is simply that many traits ascribed to the poor have not withstood empirical testing. For example, it is commonly asserted that the poor live only in the present, can't plan for or anticipate the future, and have a limited time perspective.

---

[2]It is not just the poor who demonstrate such differences. For example, crime is certainly not valued by middle- and upper-middle class Americans, yet more money was embezzled by white-collar workers in 1960 than was stolen by burglars, pickpockets, robbers, and automobile thieves (Hartung, 1969, p. 1104). And, the rate of "welfare chiseling" is generally around 5 percent, while it is estimated that about 33 percent of Americans cheat on their income taxes (Gans, 1972, p. 280, footnote 8).

However, Allen writes, "In sum, the literature review indicates that the assumption that the poor have shorter time perspective is rather untenable in light of empirical findings" (1970, pp.246-247).

Deleterious Implications of the Culture-of-Poverty Concept

Oscar Lewis and other proponents of the culture-of-poverty concept have also been criticized on the grounds that their formulation has negative implications for social action to alleviate and eradicate poverty. These critics argue—and we agree—that to stress poverty as a problem of culture is to draw attention away from the fundamental problem of poverty: the lack of economic resources. Even the staunchest supporters of Lewis' position see economic deprivation and discrimination as the root problem; the culture of poverty is an adaptation to this condition. By stressing the adaptation, however, the problem is shifted onto the shoulders of the poor, and remedial programs are aimed at changing *them* rather than the underlying socioeconomic conditions.

Focusing on the poor as the problem also diverts attention from the factors that complicate changing the socioeconomic conditions (e.g., governmental policies, mode of economic organization). One of these factors—the attitudes and beliefs of the nonpoor regarding poverty and programs—is of special interest to social psychologists. Later in this chapter we will discuss how these attitudes and beliefs impede effective movement toward reducing or eliminating poverty as a social problem.

THE STRUCTURAL DETERMINISM VIEW OF POVERTY

As the reader has probably already guessed, we feel that the culture-of-poverty explanation only touches on one part of the problem of poverty. We see poverty as primarily a problem of economic deprivation, which is rooted in the political and economic structure of society. This is not to say that being poor has no effect on those living in poverty. Indeed, as we shall shortly see, poverty has a number of social-psychological consequences. To this extent, we accept part of the culture-of-poverty formulation. What we do not accept, however, is the implication that (1) America's urban poverty is largely culturally transmitted and hence self-perpetuating, and (2) antipoverty measures that do not change cultural traits first are doomed to failure.

Our position, which we call structural determinism, has been labeled the "multidimensional conditions approach" by Will and Vater (1970), and is very clearly stated by David Matza:

> At its source, poverty is an economic matter. Especially in advanced industrial nations, its causes may be found in the existing arrangements of property and income; in the persistence of business cycles in capitalist economies, with the resultant periodic underemployment and unemployment; and in the prevailing system of public welfare that doles out approximately the demeaning assistance desired by the entrepreneurs of a disciplined and "productive" labor force. The manifestations and consequences of poverty, however, are to be found mainly among the poor themselves and . . . poverty is not especially ennobling. This does not mean . . . that I believe the poor to be the "cause" of poverty or responsible for their own condition. My actual view happens to be almost precisely the opposite. The only sense in which the poor themselves perpetuate their condition is by sometimes being so engulfed or demoralized by their situation as to be unable to effectively act against and overthrow existing arrangements or change them to their own advantage. That is a very minimal assignment of responsibility for one's own condition roughly equivalent to that properly accorded to the slave for his captivity or a people for their destruction (Matza, 1971, p. 601).

The Multidimensional Nature of Economic Deprivation

In the nineteenth century, poverty was defined in terms of some assumed level of income necessary for subsistence. Over the years, however, it has become increasingly clear that it is impossible to fix a specific minimum subsistence level. Different societies have different ideas about what a minimum subsistence entails and within a society standards change over time. Consequently, poverty is "relative to time and place" (Miller & Riessman, 1968, p. 4). For 1971, the Social Security Administration, the federal government agency responsible for "defining" poverty, set the "poverty" levels as listed in Table 3-1. The table reveals that an average family (husband, wife, and two children) not living on a farm needed an annual income of $4,137 to achieve some minimal level of existence, to be out of poverty. We can put this figure in perspective by noting two other pieces of data. First,

Table 3-1 Poverty Levels in 1971 for Nonfarm Households by Size of Family and Sex of Head

Size of family	Total	Male head*	Female head*
All unrelated individuals	$2,040	$2,136	$1,978
Under 65 years	2,098	2,181	2,017
65 years and over	1,940	1,959	1,934
All families	3,724	3,764	3,428
2 persons	2,633	2,641	2,581
Head under 65 years	2,716	2,731	2,635
Head 65 years and over	2,448	2,450	2,437
3 persons	3,229	3,246	3,127
4 persons	4,137	4,139	4,116
5 persons	4,880	4,884	4,837
6 persons	5,489	5,492	5,460
7 or more persons	6,751	6,771	6,583

*For unrelated individuals, sex of the individual.
Source: U.S. Dept. of Commerce, Current Population Reports: Consumer Income, ser. P-60, no. 82, July 1972, p. 7.

in 1966 the Bureau of Labor Statistics estimated that for an urban family of four to have "a modest but adequate standard of living" they needed an annual income of $9,191. Second, the $4,137 figure is far below what the American public feels is necessary for a minimum existence. In January of 1971, George Gallup asked a random sample of Americans "What is the SMALLEST amount of money a family of four . . . needs each week to get along in this community?" The average reply for those interviewed was $126 per week or $6,552 per year.

In 1971 over 25 million Americans (12 percent of the total population) fell below the official poverty level. Who are these poor people? Most of them are white, although a higher proportion of blacks and Spanish-speaking individuals than of whites fall below the poverty line. The rate of poverty is higher in rural areas, but in sheer numbers urban poverty is a greater problem since 56 percent of all those officially classified as poor live in or near cities. In sum, poverty is not a property of one group or area, although the highest concentrations of poverty are among blacks and other minorities in urban ghettos.

The official definition of poverty in terms of annual income underestimates the extent and depth of poverty. Economic deprivation includes lack of assets, pension reserves (to provide income when old), liquid reserves (i.e., cash on hand for emergencies), consumer durables (e.g., washing machines), and housing. Since income and the other aspects of economic well-being are generally contingent on employment, not holding a steady, well-paying job is a fundamental aspect of poverty. In sum, our multidimensional economic deprivation definition treats poverty as a relative lack of employment and income, as well as of the other components of economic well-being such as assets and housing.

THE SOCIOPSYCHOLOGICAL CONCOMITANTS OF POVERTY

In this section we will review evidence on sociological and psychological characteristics of the poor. The evidence to be reported is for the most part correlational; that is, a certain characteristic is associated with or occurs in conjunction with being poor. We choose to view *being poor* as the important variable, but this is almost impossible to prove unequivocally (see our discussion of this problem in Chapter 2).

In discussing the sociopsychological outcomes of being poor we will first cover *interpersonal* or group-level variables such as community and family cohesiveness. Next we will treat *intrapersonal* or individual-level variables. The intrapersonal variables can be further subdivided into those that are primarily psychological (personality variables) and those that are primarily physical (health, nutrition, and so on).

Poverty and Interpersonal Relations

One of the most prominent characteristics of poverty neighborhoods is the dearth of community organizations. Such organizations, which are much more prominent in middle-class areas, are designed to help the community solve problems or attain goals. Some groups are long-lasting and aimed at particular problems (e.g., the PTA); others are long-lasting but with more general goals (e.g., political parties); still others are short-lived, coming into existence to allow the community to confront a particular issue and then fading away once the issue has been decided (e.g., a group organized to stop the building of a highway through a particular neighborhood). Inner-city neighborhoods tend to have fewer of these organizations and participation is low in those that do exist. (As we shall see in a subsequent section, this pattern may be changing.) This does not mean, however, that lower socioeconomic neighborhoods are devoid of social organization. Voluntary associations (social clubs and churches, primarily) exist, but tend to be concerned with internal organizational questions rather than with the interests of the larger community.

If such organizations are desirable,[3] why haven't residents banded together more frequently? A number of factors probably contribute to the lack of such organizations. First, lower-class neighborhoods are often organized along family lines and social groups defined in terms of kinship. Such groups provide social support and interaction as well as help in emergencies. Also, the competition within the ghetto for scarce resources (especially money and social esteem) leads to much conflict and generally to suspicion among ghetto residents (Clark, 1967). [A recent study (Johnson, 1969) shows, however, that blacks are more suspicious of whites than of fellow blacks.] Finally, as we will document in the next section on individual-level variables, the poor are characterized by a low sense of personal power or efficacy. It may be that the belief that their efforts won't be fruitful causes ghetto residents to reject voluntary associations as ineffectual. Unfortunately there is no direct evidence on this latter point. There is, however, indirect evidence: persons who are higher in perceived personal power are more likely to join in organizations designed to overcome barriers to social and personal progress. For example, in the early 1960s, black college students who scored high on a measure of perceived personal power were more likely to participate in a civil rights activity than those who scored low (Gore & Rotter, 1963).

The deleterious effects of poverty are also evident at the family level. When compared with the more affluent segments of society, the poor have a higher divorce rate, a higher desertion rate, and, among

---

[3] There is good reason to believe that community organizations are desirable. For example, Blum and Rossi (1968, pp. 356–356) have provided numerous examples of the positive aspects of having such organizations and the negative impact of not having them.

those who are married, a greater level of dissatisfaction with marriage (for summaries of this research see Goode, 1971, pp. 485–503; and Blum & Rossi, 1968, pp. 368–369).[4] The exact causes of such marital instability among the poor are not yet known. However, Mitchell (1972) has offered a tentative yet plausible explanation: the poor worry about their lack of resources, which often leads to conflict between husband and wife over allocation of their limited resources. This conflict spills over into other non-money areas of family life, which in turn leads to lowered communication and interaction between spouses, making the solution of new problems or conflicts even more difficult, and adding to marital dissatisfaction. The lowered cohesiveness of the family unit, then, makes it more difficult for the family members to cope with their lack of economic resources, which brings us full circle. Though individual parts of this explanatory model have received verification (e.g., poor families do have lower rates of communication) there has as yet been no full-scale test of it.

Intrapersonal Concomitants of Being Poor

As we noted in our critique of the culture-of-poverty concept, there is much uncertainty about data concerning the distinctive individual-level traits of the poor. A number of traits often ascribed to the poor by social scientists simply do not stand the test of empirical investigation.

There are, however, certain individual-level variables on which the poor and nonpoor do differ. Again, however, two cautions are in order. First, a higher incidence of a particular trait among the poor when contrasted with the more affluent does not necessarily mean that the trait is "characteristic" of poor people. For example, we referred above to a higher incidence of marital instability among the poor; yet marital instability is not a "characteristic" of the poor, since a majority of the poor have stable marriages (stable in terms of our society's definition of stability—staying together). Second, there is great diversity among the poor (as there is at every socioeconomic level) and the generaliza-

---

[4] It is important to note that we are speaking of *differences* between groups in divorce rate, etc. "At any one point in time, most of the households in the general population *and among the poor* are intact, with both husband and wife present" (Blum & Rossi, 1968, p. 369; emphasis is added).

tions below will certainly fail to describe certain subgroups of the poor.

With these cautions in mind, what traits seem to distinguish the poor from the nonpoor? One class of variables, which we loosely call *psychological*, includes general unhappiness, low interest in and little knowledge of domestic and international affairs, and a low sense of personal efficacy. As a number of writers have pointed out, one of the primary psychological consequences of being poor is that one worries a lot and is not generally happy (Allen, 1970, p. 179; Mitchell, 1972). This fact—which is documented in numerous studies (cf. Robinson & Shaver, 1969)—may seem obvious, but it is worth noting since many affluent Americans seem to think that the poor are "contented" to be on welfare, that the unemployed are "happy that they don't have to work." Even the popular stereotype of sex among the poor—frequent, wild, and uninhibited—is contradicted; those lower in socioeconomic status reported less satisfaction from sexual behavior (Rainwater, 1966) and working-class males are more sexually active than their counterparts below the poverty line (Kinsey, 1948).

A major tenet of the American political system is that citizens are interested in and informed about their government and feel they have a say in political matters. A number of national and local surveys, however, indicate that Americans as a group feel estranged from the political system and have little knowledge about government. About 80 percent of American adults are unable to correctly identify the Bill of Rights or to name the three branches of the federal government (Lane & Sears, 1964, p. 61). Both this sense of political alienation and lack of information are particularly prominent at the bottom of the socioeconomic ladder.

The sense of political alienation is part of a more general belief that one is not personally powerful enough to influence the course of one's life. What we call a sense of personal power (ranging from a sense of little or no power up to a sense of much power) is quite similar to what Allen (1970) calls "internal versus external control": "the degree to which an individual perceives that reinforcements are contingent on or follow from his own efforts and actions (internal) versus the degree to which he believes rewards are controlled by forces outside himself—luck, chance, fate, or powerful others (external)" (p. 251). Thus we will, at times, use external control as synonymous with low perceived personal power.

In a national sample there was a significant negative correlation between socioeconomic status and perceived personal power; that is, those in the lower strata were more likely to see their outcomes as being determined by factors outside their personal control (Franklin, 1963). A similar relationship is obtained with measures of anomie ["feelings of futility and alienation" (Allen, 1970, p. 252)], a variable that we see as an outcome of the conviction that one is relatively powerless.

A recent study by Goodwin (1972) further documents the perceived powerlessness of the poor. Since this study also points up other aspects of poverty at the individual level we will cover it in some depth, postponing for a moment the specific data on powerlessness. Goodwin constructed a questionnaire that measured, among other things, the following three work orientations: "Life Aspirations," "Work Ethic," and "Lack of Confidence in Ability to Succeed in the Work World." The "Life Aspirations" orientation defines those who want what might be called the "American good life"; respondents with high scores rate "having good health," "having a nice place to live and plenty of food," *and* "having a regular job" as highly desirable. The work ethic taps the respondent's view that work is related to his identity *and* that personal effort determines one's job success or lack of it. Those who score high on the third index are indicating a specific type of felt powerlessness, powerlessness in the area of employment.

Goodwin obtained responses to his questionnaire from a large number of people with varying characteristics. Of particular interest to us are the following three groups of respondents: "long-term welfare mothers" (the average length of time on welfare was sixteen years) and their sons, "short-term welfare mothers" (average one year) and their sons, and "outer-city" mothers and their children (members of nonwelfare families living in nonghetto city neighborhoods and whose income was around $10,000 annually).

The responses to the first orientation support our earlier point that both poor and nonpoor accept certain life aspirations since (1) poor and nonpoor tended to see "a comfortable life" and "a regular job" as going together (i.e., both groups see the "good life" as comprising meaningful employment), and (2) there were no significant differences among the various groups in terms of life aspirations (i.e., the welfare mothers, long- and short-term, obtained approximately the same scores as the nonwelfare mothers). The same picture emerges in terms of the work ethic: both poor and nonpoor were equally committed to it.

When we look at the third orientation we see clear and consistent differences between the poor and nonpoor. Welfare mothers showed very low confidence in their ability to succeed while outer-city whites were higher on this measure. The impact of race on feelings of helplessness was also indicated by the results, however, as black outer-city mothers were low in confidence even though their economic position was more secure than that of the welfare mothers. Virtually the same picture emerges when we compare the responses of the sons of welfare mothers with outer-city, nonwelfare youth: there are few differences in the value placed on the good life (which includes employment) or on the work ethic, but welfare sons and outer-city black youths have less confidence in their ability to succeed. The foregoing, therefore, further demonstrates the impact of being poor (and black) on feelings of powerlessness.

The Goodwin study also gives us some insight into the determinants of such feelings. That they are at least partially transmitted through socialization—which supports the culture-of-poverty notion—is shown by the fact that there was a significant positive correlation between the scores on the third orientation of welfare mothers and of their sons. Those mothers who felt the least confident of their ability to succeed in the work world tended to have sons with similar feelings. Perceived powerlessness, however, also seems to depend on contact with the work world. A group of welfare mothers who participated in a work-training program filled out the Goodwin questionnaire once before the program began and a second time several months after it was completed. When Goodwin contrasted those who were able to find a job with those who were not, he found that those who were still unemployed after the program showed an increase in their lack of confidence. In other words, this negative encounter with the work world (training for a job but finding no position available) increased their feelings of powerlessness. The same result was obtained in a study of a work-training program for hard-core unemployed urban youths (Gurin, 1968). The youths filled out a measure of internal-external control during the training course (time 1) and again after they had been out in the work world for a while (time 2). Those youths scoring highest in external control at time 1 received the lowest wages after graduation (thereby suggesting that powerlessness has a negative effect on job success) *and* those who had the highest wages after graduation tended to score lowest in external control *at time 2.* As Gurin suggests, the relationship between job success and perceived personal power seems to be circular: high perceived personal power → job success → high perceived personal power.[5] This circular relationship suggests that providing steady, meaningful, and rewarding employment can be an effective way of reducing perceived powerlessness. This, of course, supports the structural determinism approach to eliminating poverty. That perceived powerlessness can interfere with job success means that the culture-of-poverty idea, too, must be considered in such attempts. Specifically it suggests that new jobs must be coupled with means of overcoming perceived powerlessness.

One of the most prominent aspects of being poor is the "exceptional conditions of risk for biologic insult" (Birch & Gussow, 1970, p. 9), or, to paraphrase the language on cigarette packages, "Warning: Poverty Is Dangerous to Your Health."

The poor, particularly the nonwhite poor, are at a great health disadvantage vis-à-vis their more affluent counterparts. They are more likely to die in infancy, they have a shorter life expectancy, and are more likely to experience intellectual and psychological impairment resulting from birth complications. These complications arise in part from the fact that the poor have more children at more biologically risky times of their life, but they also arise from poverty itself, specifically from insufficient diets and lack of medical care (Birch & Gussow, 1970).

HOW THE NONPOOR SEE POVERTY AND THE POOR

As we have seen, certain psychological factors make it difficult for the poor to overcome their poverty; in much the same way, the attitudes

---

[5]That lack of work can cause lowered personal power was also illustrated in an early study by Zawadzki and Lazarsfeld (1935) in which men unemployed during the depression came to feel apathetic and helpless.

and beliefs of more affluent Americans serve to perpetuate poverty as a social problem. Earlier in this chapter we described the heart of poverty: lack of economic resources, either through absence of job opportunities or employment discrimination, or some combination of both. This lack of economic resources in turn reduces access to adequate housing and medical services and produces certain sociopsychological characteristics (particularly low perceived personal power), all of which work against the poor person getting out of poverty.

To what extent does the American public accept such an explanation of being poor? The data necessary to answer this question definitively are not available. However, the evidence we have strongly suggests that Americans, and particularly nonpoor Americans, explain being poor not in terms of sociostructural factors largely beyond the individual's control but rather in terms of a *lack of effort* on the part of the poor person. That is, nonpoor Americans tend to see poverty as a failing of the individual rather than of the political and economic system in which he or she must operate (Ryan, 1971; Feagin, 1972).

Since poverty did not become a significant political issue in America until 1964, it is not surprising that pollsters did not ask their respondents directly about the cause of poverty until March of that year.[6] At that time and on four subsequent occasions (the last in June 1967) a random sample of adults was asked, "In your opinion, which is more often to blame if a person is poor—lack of effort on his own part, or circumstances beyond his control?" The responses to this question, which are presented in Table 3-2, show that by 1967 a solid 42 percent of *all* Americans laid the blame for being poor completely on the shoulders of the poor, while only 19 percent cited external circumstances. But these figures tend to underestimate the degree to which we blame the poor for their condition. First, the tendency to answer "lack of effort" increases with increased income and education (socioeconomic status): those at the top select this option 15 percent more often than those at the bottom. Thus, if we just looked at the nonpoor, the percent selecting "lack of effort" would probably be nearer 50 percent. Second, the use of the word "poor" (as with the word "needy") tends to evoke a more sympathetic response than the word

[6] In the following discussion we will draw heavily upon the work of Schlitz (1970), who compiled a very useful summary of this research.

Table 3-2   Percent Citing Various Causes for Individual Poverty, 1964–
67

Question: In your opinion, which is more often to blame if a person is poor:
lack of effort on his own part, or circumstances beyond his control?

Response	March 1964	November 1964	October 1965	December 1965	June 1967
Total	100	100	100	100	*
Lack of effort	33	30	40	40	42
Circumstances beyond control	29	31	27	29	19
Both	32	34	27	28	*
No opinion	6	5	6	3	*

*Data not available.
Source: adapted from Schiltz (1970), p. 160 and p. 176.

"welfare." For example, Americans are much more likely to agree to
spending government money to help the needy or poor than to help
those on welfare! That the nonpoor believe that people are on welfare
or work relief because of individual factors (particularly "laziness") is
further illustrated by the responses summarized in Table 3-3. During
the Depression (specifically, in 1936) Americans were willing to admit
that being out of work was not due to a lack of individual initiative;
by 1965, however, 83% of the people felt that jobs were available for
those on relief, implying that the unemployed were not working because of some personal failing.

It is not just "the rich," however, who see poverty as resulting from
the individual failings of the poor. An intensive study of the opinions
of a group of lower-middle-class working men revealed the following:

In general, there is little sympathy given to those lower in the scale,
little reference to the overpowering forces of circumstance, only
rare mention of sickness, death of a breadwinner, senility, factories
moving out of town, and so forth. The only major cause of poverty
to which no moral blame attaches is depression or "unemployment"
—but this is not considered a strikingly important cause in the minds
of respondents (Lane, 1962, p. 72).

Table 3-3 Percent Indicating that Those on Relief Could Find Work, 1936–1965

Survey date and question	Percent*	No opinion
December 1936 "Do you think the persons taken off relief will have a hard or an easy time finding work?" Percent "easy time"	24	(†)
August 1937 "Are there many persons in your community on WPA who could get jobs if they tried?" Percent "could get jobs"	55	30
April 1939 "Do you think there are any persons on relief in this community who could get jobs in private industry if they tried?" Percent "yes, there are"	69	17
November 1964 "What proportion of persons do you think are on relief for dishonest reasons: most, some, hardly any, or none?" Percent "most" or "some"	87	12
August 1965 "Do you think many people collect unemployment benefits even though they could find work?" Percent "yes, many do"	83	10

*Base excludes "no opinion."
†Not available.
Source: Schiltz (1970), p. 156.

If a large percentage, probably a majority, of the nonpoor see poverty as the result of individual factors, we are left with the question, Why? The answer seems to lie in a combination of what social psychologists call the *attribution process* together with the core American value of self-reliance. A number of social psychologists (e.g., Jones et al., 1972) have worked out a set of principles, loosely called *attribution theory*, to account for how we perceive other people. Although there are many complicated variations of attribution theory, the three principles basic to all the versions will be sufficient for our purposes: (1) humans have a need to *explain* their own and others' behavior (e.g., *"why* did he do that?"); (2) human behavior is explained either in terms of *external factors* (e.g., "he did that because someone or something forced him to") or *internal factors* (e.g., "he did that because he wanted to or because that is his nature") or some combination of both; and (3) in making an internal attribution, the perceiver considers both *ability* and *motivation* (e.g., "I know he is responsible for the behavior because he has the ability to do it and the motivation").

How do these attribution theory principles of perception apply to the views of the nonpoor regarding poverty? To begin with, people must explain poverty; they just can't say "Some people are poor, some are rich." But in seeking such an explanation why do the nonpoor focus on internal factors? Here we need to consider the American value system. Hsu (1972), after reviewing a large volume of research and theory on this topic, concluded that the core American value is *self-reliance*, which he defines as the belief that ". . . every individual is his own master, in control of his own destiny, and will advance and regress in society only according to his own efforts" (p. 250). As Hsu points out, no one is completely in charge of his own destiny, but the belief that this is so is deeply ingrained in all Americans. The American opportunity structure is quite open (especially relative to many other societies) but it is not completely open (the poor, particularly the nonwhite poor, are shut off from many avenues of advancement). Americans, however, see the structure as completely open and place a high value on self-reliance. In terms of attribution theory, then, Americans tend to have a bias toward making internal attributions. Since it is assumed that everyone has the ability to make it, those who don't must be lacking in motivation ("they are lazy"). Thus, Americans tend to make an *attributional error* by failing to recognize the external factors involved in being poor, an error caused by the core value of self-reliance, which predisposes them to make internal attributions. [It is also probable that some of the hostility toward the poor results from racial prejudice. Nonpoor, white Americans tend to see welfare as a program for blacks (Schuchter, 1968, p. 496); consequently it is likely that attitudes toward welfare and the poor in general are influenced by attitudes toward blacks.]

An interesting sidelight, which further helps to support the attribution theory explanation of views of poverty, is the case of old-age assistance. One might think that Americans would be negative toward such aid (as they are to welfare) since it runs counter to the value placed on self-reliance. But Americans realize that the aged often do not have the *ability* to care for themselves. Hence the need of the elderly is attributed to causes beyond their control, and old-age assistance is supported by Americans (Blum & Rossi, 1968, p. 395). In summary, Americans tend to support relief for the aged probably because the elderly are not seen as able to provide for themselves. The plight of the "able-bodied" poor (almost anyone who is poor and not old), however, is seen as due to their own lack of motivation. Consequently, we can expect many Americans to oppose changes in the socioeconomic structure designed to help the poor escape poverty.

PROPOSED ANTIPOVERTY MEASURES

As we indicated above, the culture-of-poverty explanation had a strong impact on the loose package of programs subsumed under the War on Poverty. These programs, most of which were administered by the Office of Economic Opportunity, sought to change the poor to make them more responsive to the opportunities that were presumably open to them. Head Start was designed to give poor children the intellectual stimulation necessary for them to take advantage of the opportunities to learn that were available in schools. The Job Corps sought not only to train ghetto youth in particular job skills but also to inculcate the work ethic and related habits necessary for occupational success (e.g., the habit of being on time). Although not all of the evidence is in, it seems that most of these programs have not been very successful (cf. Gladwin, 1967).

It is our feeling that this failure results in large part from the deficiencies of the culture-of-poverty explanation. We feel that a more appropriate war on poverty would aim at changing the American social and economic structure, since lack of economic resources is the heart of the problem of poverty. This is not the place to detail such changes, but among those that seem most necessary and promising are (1) a guaranteed minimum income for all individuals; (2) the creation and maintenance of meaningful jobs (by government action if necessary); (3) forceful government action to end discrimination, particularly in employment; (4) expanded public housing for low-income individuals, particularly housing that does not segregate the poor from the more affluent (i.e., scatter-site housing); (5) increased rapid transit lines linking present ghetto areas with urban and suburban business and industrial areas; and (6) expanded health facilities and programs (particularly those that stress preventive medicine) for ghetto areas.

Each of these aims at correcting one or more of the underlying structural factors of poverty. A guaranteed minimum income would lift the poor out of their conditions of desperate want without the policing costs or stigma of the present welfare system. Under a national income maintenance plan, people would be automatically eligible as soon as their income fell below some specified level, so that it would not be necessary for the poor to "prove" their poverty before receiving income. Nor would the agency dispensing funds have to check on this "proof." The poor would no longer be stigmatized because the program would not be just for the "down and out" (and certified as such). Also, policing costs of the present welfare system—which some estimate to be one-fifth of all welfare spending (Gladwin, 1967, p. 701)—would be drastically reduced. The creation of jobs, ending of discrimination, and increase of rapid transit would allow those presently poor to maintain themselves above the poverty line. Of these three points, the first—the direct creation of jobs—is by far the most important since the other two are meaningless unless there is a demand for workers. Rainwater (1970) has proposed that the government create jobs by making a frontal attack on other problems in American society. For example, Starr and Carlson (1968) found that inadequate sewer systems are a major cause of urban water pollution and that to repair these systems would "generate about a million man-years of work at low-skill levels and provide direct wage payments to low-skilled workers of over $2.5 billion" (Rainwater, 1970, p. 421). Expanded public housing and health facilities are intended to break the link between lack of economic resources and inadequate housing and services.

The above proposals are not new and by themselves will not completely eradicate the problem, but we think that our discussion of poverty underlines the need for such solutions. The question of how best to implement new programs and improve existing programs for change is especially important. Many of the War on Poverty programs, for example, were filled with "gimmicks" and given much publicity, which promised to solve a very big problem in a very short time. Since none of the problems of too little submit to one easy and fast solution, such publicity has added to the difficulty of achieving any success. The nonpoor hear about the programs, think a lot is being done to end poverty, and when more funds are required they ask, "Why more? I thought the problem would be solved by now." The poor, on the other hand, often do not get much direct help from the programs. For example, in the case of job training when there are no jobs available, the programs lead them up a blind alley. For both the poor and non-poor, the introduction of programs with promises of quick success serves only to increase hostility and frustration.

The major obstacles to finding sociostructural solutions are not our technology or level of economic well-being but rather the values and attitudes of Americans. The poor need a sense of personal power, as well as self-help organizations, in order to press for and take advantage of such solutions; the more affluent must learn that only structural changes can provide long-range solutions to poverty.

The poor seem to be gaining confidence and are more willing and able to organize for needed changes in our system. In part this change can be attributed to the efforts of the Office of Economic Opportunity. The doctrine of *maximum feasible participation* and the community action programs were designed to get the poor to act on their own behalf. Although the War on Poverty was not successful in ending poverty, it did promote organization among the urban poor. In the near future it is likely that community organizations will form along racial and ethnic lines (for example, the Puerto Rican group "Aspira") and welfare lines (e.g., the National Welfare Rights Organization). Caplovitz (1970) has proposed that the poor can and should organize as consumers. He begins by documenting the fact that the "poor pay more"—primarily through "fraudulent marketing practices," discrimination, and a legal system stacked against them—and then points out that the poor have a clear self-interest to protect as consumers. That such self-interest *can* produce effective organization is attested to by the success of the Consumer Education and Protective Association (CEPA) in Philadelphia. CEPA has successfully picketed stores to stop unfair practices by the sellers; it has begun to exert local political pressure for laws to protect the consumer better, particularly the ghetto resident; and it publishes a highly successful newsletter.

Such organizations will probably bring about some structural changes and will also increase members' sense of efficacy. However, more and better organizations and an increased sense of power alone will not do the job. Without broader changes there will probably be increased frustration among the poor. Such broader changes cannot be achieved without support from the more affluent. Since gaining support from majority-group middle-class Americans is also necessary for implementing the broad, structural changes suggested in other chapters, we will postpone until Chapter 8 a discussion of how such support might be achieved.

Chapter 4

City Schools Are
Two Grade Levels Behind

In this chapter and the next we will turn to two of the major institutions[1] serving the city: the public education system and the judicial system. As in the case of the problems of "too little," problems related to the functioning of the educational and judicial systems are not found only in cities; however, these two systems have especially failed the particular subgroups (i.e., minority groups and the poor) that cluster in our inner-city areas. The failure of these institutions vis-à-vis minorities and the poor have thus become "city problems."

Americans have long valued education and seen it as the prime avenue for solving a variety of social problems. However, the

---

[1] "Institutions are fairly stable social arrangements and practices through which collective actions are taken" (Knowles & Prewitt, 1969, p. 5). That is, social institutions are formal organizations that have been established to meet certain needs of the community. Among the prominent institutions in America are medical, transportation, and economic systems, as well as those to be discussed here.

American system of public education has been subjected to two recent reexaminations. The first critical review was inspired by the Russian launch of Sputnik (the first man-made earth satellite) in 1957. Many people argued that the United States had fallen behind the U.S.S.R. in technology because the schools had failed to train children properly in mathematics and the sciences. The second reassessment occurred in the mid-1960s when the lower level of academic achievement of many children in ghetto schools was brought forcefully to the attention of the general public. It is with the failure of city schools to educate ghetto children that this chapter is primarily concerned.

THE CURRENT SITUATION IN URBAN SCHOOLS

The second reassessment of American public education was prompted by evidence that the academic performance of children in inner-city schools (who are predominantly black or Spanish-speaking and overwhelmingly poor) was far below that of children in surburban schools.[2] The low academic performance of inner-city school children is evidenced in three ways: (1) they score low on measures of intellectual and academic achievement; (2) they have high dropout rates; and (3) they more often graduate from the public education system with nonacademic high school diplomas. The major nationwide study of the performance of American school children was conducted in 1965 with a roughly representative sample of all public schools, and was published one year later under the title *Equality of Educational Opportunity* (Coleman et al., 1966), popularly known as the "Coleman Report." Although a number of measures of academic achievement were used in this study, "reading comprehension" is generally regarded as the most important, since reading ability is necessary for learning in most academic subjects and is highly correlated with other achievement measures. Reading comprehension scores demonstrated two things: (1) white Americans, regardless of region or urban-nonurban background, do well and achieve about equally; and (2) blacks, Mexican Americans, and Puerto Ricans do quite poorly and *they get*

---

[2] A number of commentators (e.g., Silberman, 1971) have asserted that *all* schools are failing their students; alienation and protest are prominent even among suburban middle-class children. The focus of the present chapter, however, is the special failure of urban schools, which do not provide inner-city children with the basic skills for adulthood.

further behind with each year in school. For example, blacks in the northeastern urban areas are 1.8 years behind their white counterparts in the sixth grade, 2.6 years behind in the ninth grade, and 2.9 years behind in the twelfth grade.

On a national level, then, the average minority-group child (particularly black and Spanish-speaking) living in an urban center (generally in a ghetto *barrio*) scores poorly on tests of academic achievement. This point is even more dramatically made if we look at the New York public school system. A group of "ghetto schools" (i.e., where enrollment is at least 95 percent black and/or Puerto Rican) was compared with a group of "nonghetto schools" (i.e., at least 83 percent white), revealing that pupils in ghetto schools were far behind their grade level in reading achievement. For example, only 10 percent of the ghetto school pupils were reading at or above grade level while 65 percent of the students in nonghetto schools were at this level (Wilkerson, 1970).

Another aspect of the urban school problem is the high dropout rate. In New York City, for example, of those students who enter the tenth grade, blacks and Puerto Ricans are almost four times as likely to drop out before the twelfth grade as are other children. And those ghetto youths who do make it through the twelfth grade are much more likely than other children to graduate with a nonacademic degree. Again in New York City, ghetto schools grant more *general* diplomas than *academic* diplomas while the reverse pattern holds for nonghetto schools. Such general diplomas indicate simply that the student attended school for the required period, and are not regarded very highly by college officials or employers (Wilkerson, 1970, p. 24). The lowered achievement, high dropout rates, and paucity of meaningful diplomas paint a picture of noneducation in ghetto schools.

REASONS FOR THE NONEDUCATION OF GHETTO CHILDREN

A number of reasons have been offered for the poor academic performance of students in inner-city schools. Some have argued that genetic factors may cause certain students (i.e., blacks) to be less capable of learning than others. This view, most often linked to

Arthur Jensen (1969), will not be discussed here. Even though genetic factors are obviously important in determining intellectual capability, it is the authors' judgment that (1) there is little evidence that such factors vary with racial or social class distinctions (i.e., that certain races are inherently "smarter" than others); (2) there is at present no sure way of separating genetic from environmental influence on "intelligence" tests and academic performance, and we know that ghetto environments (schools included) are radically different from those in middle-class suburbs; and (3) genetic theories give us almost no help in planning social change to improve conditions in urban schools. (A technical but thoroughly readable discussion of these points can be found in Goldsby, 1971.)

A second view—variously labeled *cultural deprivation, cultural disadvantage*, and *intellectual deprivation*—explains the school failure of ghetto children in terms of their lower-class culture, which purportedly does not prepare them for school and serves to weaken the effects of school. According to the cultural deprivation hypothesis, which is simply a component of the more general culture-of-poverty theory covered in the preceding chapter, the ghetto child's culture, particularly within the family, is to blame for the child's lack of school achievement. There is no doubt that the family is an important determinant of a child's orientation toward learning and of his capitalization on what he is exposed to in school. For example, a family that reinforces a child's demonstration of what he has learned is more likely to produce an academically motivated child than one in which the child's school achievements are ignored or treated as "showing off." There is also some reason to believe that children of lower socioeconomic status have fewer opportunities to talk with their parents, especially in informal situations such as mealtimes (Deutsch, 1967).

But to place the responsibility of lowered school achievement on the lower-class parents has three major drawbacks (beyond the criticism of the more general culture-of-poverty formulation discussed in Chapter 3): (1) there is dramatic evidence that schools *can* make a difference in the performance of lower-class children (cf. Clark, 1967); (2) the cultural deprivation explanation provides a ready excuse for teachers, school administrators, and other educationists, thus diverting attention from factors in the school that contribute to poor achievement; and (3) the cultural deprivation hypothesis, like genetic explanations, offers very little in the way of solutions.[3] Consequently, our major focus will not be on the ghetto child's culture, although some factors within it will be considered.

A third explanation of the poor performance of inner-city children concerns the schools they attend; it is on the failures of these schools that we will focus. We chose to do so because we feel that schools do have a significant (and, in many current instances, negative) impact on the performance of ghetto children, and schools—though not easily moved—are more amenable to change than either genetic factors or family structures.

Although the educational system is highly complex and subject to a variety of influences, its heart is the teacher and the students in the elementary and secondary public school classroom. Thus, we will cover the urban school teacher, the ghetto school child, and their special interaction pattern in order to discover why inner-city school children are doing so poorly. We will structure our discussion around three questions: (1) What are the attitudes, values, etc., that the child brings to school? (2) Who are the teachers? (3) What is the student-teacher relationship? Before attempting to answer these questions, however, we will take a brief look at the urban school itself.

The Inner-city School

Two things stand out when we consider the kind of school the ghetto child attends: (1) the physical plant is old, underequipped, and generally uninviting; and (2) the school is segregated along racial and social class lines (i.e., most students attending inner-city schools are from minority-group and/or poor families).

Since many manufacturing and service industries have left the city centers and much of the white middle class has departed in order to

---

[3] The cultural deprivation theory suggests two major types of intervention: (1) wipe out the poverty that generates and perpetuates the "detrimental" home environments and (2) reach children before they enter school to counteract the "detrimental" home environments. The first suggestion is commendable, but implementation (especially in the near future) is doubtful. The second suggestion has been tried in the form of the various Head Start projects. These programs seem to be able to raise student achievement initially but the early gains disappear as the child moves through the public school system (Goldberg, 1971, p. 79). So again, our attention is centered on existing ghetto schools.

avoid conflict and seek comfort in the suburbs, the large urban school districts have lost much of the tax base necessary to operate and maintain their schools adequately. One way in which funds have been conserved is by cutting back on new school building and retaining older school structures.

There are other ways in which the schools in low-income areas of the city are generally worse off than those attended by more affluent students. In one of the more thorough studies on this question, Patricia Sexton (1961) found that the schools attended by lower-income students (1) were located in older and inferior buildings, (2) had fewer "extras" (e.g., specialized educational and recreational facilities), and (3) had less materials and equipment. Nevertheless, although these inadequacies of slum schools may well contribute to the inferior performance of the children who attend them, the effect is probably smaller than one might first guess. The Coleman Report, for example, found only small and somewhat inconsistent differences (within each geographical region) between the physical and material quality of schools attended by whites and blacks. And, by itself, the physical quality of the school had little impact on the achievement scores of the children attending the school. The foregoing should not suggest that existing inequities in physical plant and materials need not be remedied, but that simply spending more money to increase the physical accoutrements of urban schools will not produce the greatest yield in terms of raising pupil achievement.

One of the most characteristic and significant qualities of American public education is that it is segregated. The Coleman Report demonstrated that no matter what the region or the size of the city, whites and blacks generally attended separate schools. Among first-graders in 1965, for example, 65 percent of the black children attended schools with over 90 percent black enrollment and 80 percent of the white children were in schools that were at least 90 percent white. Subsequent analysis of the Coleman Report data demonstrated that racial segregation is even greater in the large urban areas than in the nation as a whole.

The extent of racial segregation in our cities is illustrated in Table 4-1. In all ten of these major cities, 50 percent or more of the black students attended schools in which blacks were a majority and in most cities blacks attended almost all-black schools and whites attended

Table 4-1   Extent of Segregation in Public Schools in Ten Major Cities,
1965-66 School Year

	Percent of total Negro elementary students in schools 90-100 percent Negro	Percent of total Negro elementary students in majority Negro schools	Percent of total White elementary students in schools 90-100 percent white
New York	20.7	55.5	56.8
Chicago	89.2	96.9	88.8
Los Angeles	39.5*	87.5*	94.7*
Philadelphia	72.0	90.2	57.7
Detroit	72.3	91.5	65.0
Baltimore	84.2	92.3	67.0
Houston	93.0	97.6	97.3
Cleveland	82.3†	94.6†	80.2†
Washington	90.4	99.3	34.3
St. Louis	90.9	93.7	66.0

*1963-64 data
†1962-63 data
Italic type indicates school population is more than 40 percent black.
Source: Adapted from Schuchter (1968), pp. 238-239.
Original Source: Alsop (1967). Copyright © 1967 by Joseph Alsop.

almost all-white schools. Two of the more extreme examples—Chicago
(where 89.2 percent of the black students attended almost all-black
schools) and St. Louis (where 90.9 percent of the black students
attended such schools)—indicate that the problem of school segregation
is not limited to the South.

   There are a number of reasons why *de facto* segregated education
exists. First, as we indicated in Chapter 1, blacks are becoming more
and more concentrated in city centers. Second, there is little coopera-
tion between suburban and urban school districts. Third, within urban
school districts whites often attend private schools; in Philadelphia,
for example, about 60 percent of the white school children attend
private schools. Fourth, segregation within urban school districts is
maintained by building new facilities in all-white or all-black neighborhoods, by carefully drawing the school boundaries to maintain racial
homogeneity, and so on. (For a fuller discussion of these points, see
Pettigrew, 1971, pp. 56-57.)

   Whatever the reasons for segregated school systems, the Coleman

Report demonstrates that it does have effects on performance. One of the major correlates of academic performance was "social class climate" of the school. More specifically, all students tended to do better if they attended a school where the students were predominantly of middle-class background (see Pettigrew, 1971, p. 58). As Pettigrew goes on to point out, social class segregation is significant for minority groups because they tend to be overrepresented in lower socioeconomic levels. Even more to the point, the Coleman Report showed that blacks attending desegregated schools *with at least 50 percent white enroll-ment* scored higher on achievement tests than those in predominantly black schools. And, the performance of whites in these schools was no lower than in comparable schools without black students.

Thus desegregation seems to improve minority-group school achievement; but desegregation is not enough. Of the desegregated schools as defined above, some were characterized by interracial tension while others reported no such tension and students had more interracial friendships. The black students attending schools of this latter type, which we will call *integrated* schools, had higher verbal achievement scores than those attending schools that were simply desegregated.[4]

Other research has shown that truly integrated situations (in industry, neighborhoods, etc., as well as schools) must involve minority- and majority-group members working, on an equal status and a cooperative basis, toward common goals (Ashmore, 1970, pp. 318–337). Thus, to achieve integration we must do more than simply mix black and white school children together in the same school. For example, any form of hard-and-fast grouping (either between or within classes) that tends to divide black and white children will also preclude the opportunity for interracial cooperative activity. Not only should such forms of "ability" grouping be ended (see also the subsequent section in this chapter on the self-fulfilling prophecy) and replaced with desegregated and changing groupings of children, but also reading and other within-class groupings should stress cooperative goals rather than academic competition, as is the current practice.

Not only does truly integrated education appear to enhance the

---

[4]The Coleman Report—and especially its treatment of the social class climate variable—has received much criticism (see, for example, Dyer, 1968). Our interpretation of the report is most congruent with that of Thomas F. Pettigrew (1971, pp. 57–69).

educational advancement of minority-group children; it can also reduce intergroup hostility and prejudice. The design specified above for true integration (i.e., equal-status contact on a cooperative basis and in pursuit of common goals) has been shown to promote interracial or intergroup friendships, which in turn serve to reduce intergroup prejudice (Ashmore, 1970). Thus, integrated education offers the promise of enhancing the educational achievement of minority-group children. And, as a side benefit, it can also operate to decrease intergroup hostility.

The foregoing analysis suggests that school desegregation should be a prime ingredient of any program to improve urban education. Such a conclusion would not have seemed too surprising a decade ago. Today, a number of prominent minority-group leaders are arguing that integration is less important than quality education, even if the latter remains separate. Our feeling is that integration and quality education within inner-city schools are neither antagonistic nor mutually exclusive goals (see also Clark, 1967, p. 117) and that both must be sought. We further believe together with Miller and Riessman (1968, pp. 142–145), that quality-segregated education does not hold much promise as a long-range strategy for improving the education of large numbers of minority-group children.

Even if one accepts the goal of integrated education, the question remains of how to end *de facto* segregation. Pettigrew (1971, pp. 69–80) has offered a general plan. For small and relatively compact school districts he recommends busing, the redrawing of school boundaries, the pairing of black and white schools in order to exchange students, and other similar means of redistributing children among schools. In such a redistribution it is important that the burden of movement not fall only on the minority-group children. The busing-in of minority children tends to stigmatize them and to put them under much psychological stress (Chesler et al., 1968). The best way to equalize the burden would seem to be desegregation on a systemwide basis that involves busing—where necessary—of both majority-group and minority-group pupils. Such a plan was instituted in Berkeley, California, and to date it seems to be working quite well (Gentry et al., 1972, pp. 42–46).

For larger school districts Pettigrew recommends *educational parks*. These would be large campuses (similar to a college campus), each with several elementary schools and a smaller number of intermediate and high schools. The parks would be constructed in an area between the inner-city ghetto and outlying suburbs, and near rapid transit lines that would allow easy access to and from ghetto and suburb alike. The educational park concept has much to recommend it: not only could it serve to reduce segregation, but in the long run it could also reduce costs (though the initial outlay, of course, would be quite large) by allowing the consolidation of dining and other facilities.

In recent years, however, there have been numerous instances of voters turning down bond issues to finance school improvements, and the large initial expense, in addition to the racial issue, would probably make voters resistant to the educational park concept. In Chapter 8 we will attempt to provide at least a preliminary answer to the problem of overcoming such resistance.

WHAT THE GHETTO CHILD BRINGS TO SCHOOL

In psychological research a distinction is usually made between two general types of variables that account for behavior. The first type is comprised of the attitudes, values, beliefs, and other internal predispositions to behave in certain ways; these are called individual-difference variables, or, more generally, "what the individual brings to the situation." The second type is made up of situational environmental factors that impinge on the individual. In this section we will look at what the inner-city school child brings with him or her and examine how these individual-difference factors influence the educational process.

In discussions about the cause of the low achievement levels in ghetto schools the following explanations often come up: "They come from a culture that doesn't value education"; "They have a negative attitude toward teachers and schools"; "They aren't motivated to do well in school." In other words "they" (minority-group and other poor children) develop in the home certain negative attitudes and values regarding education, and their negativism makes it difficult to teach them. Although this view may apply to some inner-city children, it certainly does not seem valid for the great majority of them. For example, Cloward and Jones (1963) found in a survey of parents living on the lower East Side of New York that at least 95 percent of all parents in all social classes agreed that "a good education is essential to getting ahead." Moreover, lower-class parents did not have a more negative attitude toward the particular schools their children attended than middle-class parents. They did feel, however, that the schools did not pay enough attention to the needs of children from poor families. Thus, these parents of inner-city school children valued education as much as more affluent members of society, but their view of the schools, while not more negative in general, reflected the particular unmet needs of their children.

Minority-group children themselves also place a high value on education, as is indicated by several findings of the Coleman Report. When asked what kind of student they wished to be, 48 percent of black and 36 percent of Puerto Rican children in the metropolitan Northeast answered "one of the best students in the class." This is especially impressive when one notes that this same response was given by 36 percent of the white children in the region. And, although whites were somewhat more likely to want to finish college than blacks, 86 percent of both groups wanted to obtain some form of education beyond high school. The black children were more likely to want to go to some type of technical school, which was a very realistic goal in light of the job opportunities and rewards available to them. In Chapter 3, we discussed job discrimination and its psychological implications. Here we need only note that such discrimination makes each year of schooling *less important* (in terms of leading to a higher-paying job) for nonwhites than for whites. In 1966, for example, the median yearly income for a white male with an elementary school education was $3,731 and for a nonwhite $2,362; the figures for whites and nonwhites with a high school education were $6,736 and $4,725, respectively, and following college the figures were $9,023 and $5,928, respectively. Thus, not only do whites earn more than blacks at every educational level, but *the gap between the races increases at every level, especially after college* (Sears & McConahay, 1973, p. 51). It is quite rational, then, for blacks and other ghetto children to seek a relatively short technical training program rather than college and postgraduate study, since each year of schooling means less for them than for whites in terms of future income.[5]

_____

[5] This should not be taken to mean that blacks don't want to attend college or that blacks pick technical schools simply because it is a rational choice (see Cicourel & Kituse, 1963, for a discussion of how high school guidance counselors push blacks and other minorities into such choices).

If educational aspirations do not on the whole distinguish the ghetto child from his counterparts in white middle- and upper-class neighborhoods, what individual-level variables do? A large number of "personality traits" have been attributed to the disadvantaged child (see particularly Deutsch, 1967), but much of the research involved is contradictory or inconclusive. Therefore, we will consider only those factors that we feel have been clearly demonstrated and that have direct implications for the way in which inner-city schools treat (or should treat) their pupils. First, as was indicated in Chapter 3, the poor child—and particularly the poor nonwhite child—is more likely than the white middle-class child to bring medical and nutritional problems to school. These health problems of the poor influence school performance both directly and indirectly (Birch & Gussow, 1970). Undernutrition, overexposure to illness and accident, and lack of access to decent medical care can directly affect learning ability by producing neurological damage. At least as important, however, are the indirect effects of the poor health of the ghetto child; in particular, loss of learning time (a frequently sick child simply has less time to study) and changes in both motivation and personality. As we all know, being sick makes us more irritable and chronic illness can lead to apathy. A ghetto child's apparent lack of interest in classroom activities may also result from the anemia which is often associated with poor diet. In sum, improper diets and lack of proper medical care can make the inner-city child less able (and less motivated) to learn in school. Again, a full attack on school failure requires attention to outside factors—in this case, health care for the poor, and poverty itself.

In addition, the ghetto child often enters school using a language different from that of his teachers and from that which he is expected to master while in school. This language difference is most clearly seen in the case of Mexican-American or Puerto Rican youth, whose native tongue may be a dialect of Spanish. It is no less true, however, that many inner-city black children—and some white (for example, those moving to Chicago and other Midwest cities from isolated Appalachian communities)—enter school most familiar with a language system that differs from the one they will be expected to learn. One of the best studied of these languages, known as *Negro nonstandard English* or *black dialect,* is interpreted by many teachers and some researchers simply as an inferior or deficient form of standard English. Such an interpretation is logical in a sense because Negro nonstandard English is quite similar to standard English (see Table 4-2).

A number of linguists, however, have clearly demonstrated that black dialect is a different, yet fully as effective, system of communication as the more standard brand of English spoken in most suburbs

Table 4.2 Some Syntactic Differences between Negro Nonstandard and Standard English

Variable	Standard English	Negro nonstandard
Linking verb	He *is* going	He . . . goin'
Possessive marker	John*'s* cousin	John . . . cousin
Plural marker	I have five cent*s*	I got five cent . . .
Subject expression	John . . . lives in New York	John *he* live in New York
Verb form	I *drank* the milk	I *drunk* the milk
Past marker	Yesterday he *walked* home	Yesterday he walk . . . home
Verb agreement	He run*s* home She *has* a bicycle	he run . . . home She *have* a bicycle
Future form	I *will go* home	*I'ma go* home
"If" construction	I asked *if he did it*	I ask *did he do it*
Negation	I *don't* have *any* He *didn't* go	I *don't* got *none* He *ain't* go
Indefinite article	I want *an* apple	I want *a* apple
Pronoun form	*We* have to do it *His* book	*Us* got to do it *He* book
Preposition	He is over *at* his friend's house He teaches *at* Francis Pool	He over *to* his friend house He teach . . . Francis Pool
Be	Statement: He *is here all the time*	Statement: *He be here*
Do	Contradiction: No, *he isn't*	Contradiction: No, he *don't*

Source: Baratz (1970), pp. 16–17.

(see particularly Williams, 1970).[6] In saying that black dialect is an effective system of communication we mean that it allows the black child to communicate with those in his neighborhood, and this is the prime function of language. Furthermore, this dialect is just as useful for thinking about and solving complex mental problems as standard English. The charge that black dialect is worse (or better) than any other for thinking purposes simply does not hold.

Up to this point we have spoken as if there were just one black dialect. In fact, however, there are many different nonstandard English dialects spoken by black Americans. Charles Valentine (1971), for example, records six such black dialects of English (as well as eight other black dialects of French or Spanish) and future research will probably uncover others. Valentine makes another significant point about the language of black Americans. In criticizing both the deficit theory and the difference theory he argues that most black Americans have some knowledge of both standard English and one or more black dialects. (They are exposed through television and other mass media to standard English while they acquire their nonstandard dialect in interaction within their neighborhood subculture.) Thus, the black school child should not be treated as totally without standard English. Rather, each child's skills in standard English and black dialect must be ascertained and used in teaching the child further skills.

The foregoing points regarding language use among minority children, particularly blacks, have important implications for urban education. As we shall see in a subsequent section of this chapter, the use of a nonstandard dialect is one of the cues that guide many teachers in classifying children as slow learners and assigning them to a low group for reading. That is, many urban teachers operate on an implicit deficit theory of language; they assume that use of a particular language has implications for language and reasoning ability.

Our analysis suggests several changes in teacher training and classroom curriculum that would improve the education of minority-group children, First, teacher training programs—especially those preparing teachers for urban classrooms—should include linguistics training in

---

[6] Here it should be noted that standard English is more of a goal than a reality. Most white Americans speak some variant or dialect of standard English. There is only one situation in which standard English is consistently spoken: network television newscasts.

how to identify nonstandard English. Second, nonstandard English dialects can be used to teach standard English.[7] A number of such programs have been developed [e.g., use of ethnic readers (Baratz & Shuy, 1969), teaching standard English as a second language (John & Horner, 1970)] and only intensive research will indicate which is the most effective under various conditions for different types of children.

For many years psychologists and educators have seen low self-esteem (i.e., a negative view of one's value, worth, or ability) among black children as probably important in causing low school achievement. The argument was quite plausible: (1) a number of studies made in the 1940s and 1950s suggested that black children, presumably because they occupied a lower social position in American society, had lower self-esteem than whites of the same age (e.g., Clark & Clark, 1947; Stevenson & Stewart, 1958); (2) those who think they are not very competent probably don't try as hard as those who think well of themselves; (3) this reduced effort leads to inferior outputs; and (4) negative teacher comments and poor grades reinforce the child's initial sense of worthlessness.

In their review of research on this question, however, Backman and Secord (1968) found a very mixed picture of results; some studies find self-esteem and school achievement positively correlated, others do not, and still others find one relationship for boys and a different one for girls. The previously mentioned Coleman Report provides an interesting suggestion about the relationship between self-concept and school performance. In the Coleman data, high academic performance for white children is more closely associated with a positive "academic self-concept" (i.e., high self-esteem regarding academics) while for black students a sense of personal power (e.g., feeling that "hard work" is more important for success than "good luck") is more strongly associated with good grades. Thomas F. Pettigrew (1971) uses this data to speculate that there is a two-step process relating self-concept to achievement. The first step is for children to learn that personal effort is related to outcomes (rewards and punishment) and the second step

---

[7]Some have argued that in a truly pluralistic society one should not force one language on all children (see Wrightsman, 1972, p. 252). Our feeling, however, is that an approximation of standard English is necessary for educational and occupational success and that fluency in standard English should be developed in all American children. *This does not mean, however, that minority-group children should be required to give up or deny their particular dialect.*

is for them to learn to evaluate their efforts positively. Several other studies find that perceived personal power (also known as internal control or personal efficacy) is predictive of higher academic performance among minority children (see Backman & Secord, 1968, pp. 76–77; Wittes, 1970, pp. 26–29).

The above is congruent with our finding in Chapter 3 that lack of perceived personal power is an important characteristic of poor people. It also suggests that programs aimed at improving perceived personal power will not only enhance school achievement but also will have a positive effect on later job performance. Only one such program has been developed and even this one not fully (deCharms, 1972). The initial results, however, are quite impressive and they warrant follow-up research.

As the foregoing suggests (and it is even more obvious in other treatments of the "disadvantaged" child) most research on what the ghetto child brings to school has focused on weakensses or deficits. There is some evidence, however, that the ghetto child often possesses a number of potential strengths on which the schools fail to capitalize. The following essay, reproduced exactly as the child wrote it, illustrates this point:

> Since I was about 7 years old I began work around the house, such as washing dishes, sweeping the floor and going to the store. I did these things mostly because I asked. Sometimes my mother was not home to teach me so I had to learn myself. Then I began to like it some much that it became a habit finally a job. This job was like any other job only you didn't get paid for it. While doing my work if I did something wrong I would get yelled at, hit, or sometimes beaten. As I grew older I learned about things that you had to careful with such as matches, ironing and gas. A few years later I knew how to fold things like shirts very well, as the years went by the job became boring so gragarily I lost some of my skills. Up till now I still do the same jobs but there are things added, baby-sitting (Rosenfeld, 1971, p. 87).

This essay suggests two potential strengths of the ghetto child: he is active rather than passive, and he is capable of individual initiative and responsibility. Although these personality traits are certainly valued by Americans, little has been done to utilize them constructively in the urban classroom. In fact, the tough independence of many ghetto children often intimidates, frightens, and annoys their teachers, especially those fresh from a teacher training program. As we will see in the section on urban teachers, one way to improve ghetto education is to prepare teachers better so they can understand and deal with the children they will be called upon to teach. In addition, there are two other promising ways of capitalizing on the strengths of many ghetto children. First, their active style and individual responsibility can be put to use by having older children help younger ones with their lessons. Miller and Riessman (1968) call this the *helper principle* and they cite numerous successful applications of it. In one case the reading scores of both the helper and the helped youngsters were improved. Not only does the helper principle promise to increase the academic performance of those involved, but it would also help free the teacher, who is generally overburdened, *and* probably increase the helper's sense of personal power. Second, recent advances in computer technology open up the possibility of children learning at their own pace using computer consoles (where the child "talks" with the computer). These advances (broadly classed under the rubric *computer-assisted instruction*), which will be discussed in the section on teachers, may be particularly significant in urban classrooms since they require a very active role on the part of the learner, i.e., the student *interacts with* the computer instead of *listening to* the teacher.

In sum, we have seen that the ghetto child brings to school a number of personal characteristics that have implications for his education. Contrary to the culture-of-poverty and cultural-deprivation theories, however, not all these characteristics are deficits. They are mainly *differences* (for example, language) some of which are strengths that up to now have generally been ignored or misinterpreted (for example, high activity level may be seen as a problem rather than a resource). It is the responsibility of the educational system to understand differences and utilize strengths, and not to convert all the urban child's characteristics into deficits.

THE URBAN SCHOOL TEACHER

Just as the factors that the pupil brings to the educational setting are important determinants of what and how much is learned, so too are the personal or individual qualities of the teacher. Much research has been done to uncover the demographic, personality, and intellectual characteristics of teachers, especially those associated with effective teaching (e.g., Getzels & Jackson, 1963). Our purpose here is not to cover this entire literature but rather to discuss a limited number of teacher variables which have been shown to be of importance in understanding the particular problems of urban education.

The first thing to note at this point is that inner-city schools are often understaffed with regard to regularly certified teachers, even though there is a huge surplus of such teachers nationwide. To take up the slack, ghetto schools employ significant numbers of uncertified newcomers and "old-timers" who have "adapted." Using unstructured interviews with sixty public school teachers in Chicago, Howard Becker (1952) found that since few could move up in the school hierarchy (by becoming a principal or other administrator) teachers tended to further their career by moving to the easiest types of teaching in a middle-class school. Consequently inner-city schools experience a high turnover of teachers and must usually replace those who leave with young, inexperienced, and often untrained teachers. Becker also found that those who stayed in inner-city schools relaxed the demands and expectations they had for their pupils. As we shall see, when expectation is lowered, achievement goes down.

Teachers who do start their teaching careers at an inner-city school, whether or not they have completed a formal teacher training program, bring with them many qualities that interfere with effective teaching. First, some teachers are simply prejudiced against the social class or ethnic group to which the children they are to teach belong (cf. Knowles & Prewitt, 1969, pp. 42-43). Second, and more significant since it applies to more of them, teachers see one of their prime goals— if not *the* prime goal—as the mediation of culture. And their definition of American culture is often quite restricted, involving "correct" language, a history of the United States and the world that underestimates the role of minority groups, and in general little appreciation for various ethnic and social-class subcultures. Consequently, the culture they wish to pass on often has little personal meaning for the ghetto child (which tends to make the child "turn off" and ultimately drop out). Even more detrimental, however, the teacher's insistence on passing on *the* culture serves to derogate many aspects of the ghetto child's own particular subculture. This, in turn, may cause the child to lower his own self-esteem and/or reject the school.

A third characteristic of many new teachers in inner-city schools is that they are generally unprepared for the task that confronts them. This unpreparedness, which is really a consequence of the first two characteristics, is illustrated by Herbert Kohl's description of his first meeting with his class in a Harlem school:

> The children entered at nine and filled up the seats. They were silent and stared at me. It was a shock to see thirty-six black faces before me. No preparation helped. It is one thing to be liberal and talk, another to face something and learn that you're afraid.
>
> The children sat quietly, expectant. *Everything must go well: we must like each other . . . .*
>
> "Write about yourselves, tell me who you are." (I hadn't said who I was, too nervous.)
>
> Slowly they set to work, the first directions followed—and if they had refused?
>
> Then arithmetic, the children working silently, a sullen, impenetrable front. *To talk to them, to open them up this first day.*
>
> "What would you like to learn this year? My name is Mr. Kohl."
>
> Silence, the children looked up at me with expressionless faces, thirty-six of them crowded at thirty-five broken desks. *This is the smartest class?*
>
> *Explain: they're old enough to choose, enough time to learn what they'd like as well as what they have to.*
>
> Silence, a restless movement rippled through the class. *Don't they understand? There must be something that interests them, that they care to know more about . . . .*
>
> No response. The weight of Harlem and my whiteness and strangeness hung in the air as I droned on, lost in my righteous monologue. The uproar turned into sullen silence. A slow nervous drumming began at several desks; the atmosphere closed as intelligent faces lost their animation (Kohl, 1968, pp. 13–15).

This passage not only illustrates how unprepared Kohl was for his teaching assignment but also (1) how easy it is for the teacher to attribute the failure of the teacher-pupil interaction to pupil characteristics (Kohl's question to himself: "This is the smartest class?") and (2) how easy it is to cope with the strained pupil-teacher relationship by using authority (Kohl simply said "Write about yourself," and they did) and routine (". . . I droned on, lost in my righteous monologue.") To improve teacher performance in ghetto schools, then, teachers must be prepared for the special problems of teaching in an urban classroom *and* they must be helped while on the job not to take the easy way out (i.e., to rely simply on authority and routine to keep the students quiet and busy).

Even teachers who complete a teacher training program are often not prepared for the realities of the urban classroom. This is because many teacher training programs assume that teaching is a unitary phenomenon—a single set of skills—which can be applied to any group of learners under any set of circumstances. As many who train teachers are beginning to learn, this assumption is simply not true. Although we are just beginning to experiment with and evaluate various programs for training teachers specifically for urban classrooms, several ingredients have already been shown to be important. First, since most teachers are from middle-class white backgrounds and their pupils in inner-city schools are usually nonwhite and poor, the prospective teacher has special difficulties to overcome. He will have to confront his own racial and social-class stereotypes and should therefore receive training to help him understand the cultural variations he will be likely to encounter. A group of social psychologists has recently developed a technique called the "culture assimilator" which helps a person of one culture learn about a different culture (Fiedler, Mitchell, & Triandis, 1971). At present culture assimilators have been developed only for Americans going to foreign countries but there is no reason why one could not be constructed to introduce middle-class whites to the various cultures of inner-city areas. Second, training in nonstandard dialects and how they can be employed to teach standard English is particularly important. Third, the prospective teacher must be taught how to recognize the special problems of an urban environment (e.g., how to tell if a child is suffering from anemia rather than from boredom). Finally, *and most important*, prospective teachers must have a great deal of experience in urban classrooms (at first just observing, then taking partial responsibility for the class, and finally being totally responsible for the class). This experience should be coordinated with seminars involving teacher trainees along with experienced and sensitive teachers. Several programs incorporating these ideas have already begun (e.g.,

Kornberg, 1963); while they appear to be promising, there is little direct evidence available regarding their effectiveness.

One final fact about teachers—especially those in inner-city schools—must be noted: in general they are overburdened. Not only are they expected to teach thirty or forty or more children (with varying needs and abilities) but they are also called upon to do a large amount of clerical work (e.g., keep records, fill out forms). There are several ways to relieve overburdened teachers and thus head off their tendency to become more control-oriented the longer they stay on the job. First, there is need for significant increases in on-the-job or in-service training for teachers. This does not mean taking a course during summer vacation or at night school. Rather it means taking time off from class during the school year to meet with educators and other active teachers to explore and evaluate one's own style of teaching. Second, several alternatives are available for easing the teacher's job within the classroom. As mentioned earlier, older children could be employed to help younger children. Also parents and paraprofessionals could take over certain classroom responsibilities. (This would have the side benefit of increasing community involvement in the school.) Finally, computers could be employed to provide individualized instruction in certain subjects.

A wide variety of approaches has been suggested for using computers in education (see, for example, Hammond, 1972) but one of the most promising for upgrading ghetto education was developed by Patrick Suppes and his associates (Suppes & Morningstar, 1970). They have worked out a way of freeing the teacher by using the computer for drill-and-practice sessions. Although most of their work has been on systems for arithmetic, other programs are being developed for foreign languages and reading. The system involves a teletype, a typewriterlike device, which allows the respondent to communicate with a computer situated in an isolated part of the classroom. Each day the student has an "appointment" with the teletype. He types in his name and identification number and the computer responds by typing back the student's first problem to solve. If the student makes a mistake the computer replies NO, TRY AGAIN and the problem is typed again. If the student repeats his error the correct answer is given by the computer and the student is asked to rework the problem. At the end of the day's session the student takes with him his sheet of problems and answers (along with a summary score) to keep for later reference.

This procedure is based on a number of principles for effective learning that have long been recognized by psychologists (cf. Suppes & Morningstar, 1970, p. 225). For example, the child gets immediate feedback as to whether his response is correct. Thus, he can clearly tell when he is right and maintain the response; he also knows when he is wrong and that he must try to find a better response.

The research conducted by Suppes and others using similar apparatus indicates that such computer-assisted instruction is as effective as similar drill-and-practice conducted by a skilled and conscientious teacher. Thus, the computer could effectively be used to free the teachers from such responsibilities. Also, the computerized drill-and-practice allows each student to move at his own pace. "Slower" students are not stigmatized for holding up the class and "faster" students are not frustrated by the teacher's need to explain certain things to the rest of the class. In sum, computer-assisted drill-and-practice has much to recommend it. However, the realities of implementing such instruction on a broad scale must not be ignored: computers are very expensive and, to reduce the cost, much cooperative sharing of computer time within and between school systems must be arranged. Also, school systems—like other bureaucracies—are resistant to change.

Teacher–Student Interaction in the Classroom:
The Self-fulfilling Prophecy and School Failure

Probably the greatest contribution of psychologists to understanding the failure of urban education has been their research on the self-fulfilling prophecy. The most widely known work in this area is *Pygmalion in the Classroom* (Rosenthal & Jacobson, 1968). It is the report of a field experiment that demonstrated that teacher expectancies of how a pupil will perform can influence how the pupil actually performs even if the original expectancy was not based on the pupil's actual or potential ability. That is, the teacher's expectation or prophecy somehow causes the expectation to come true, hence the term *self-fulfilling prophecy.*

Pygmalion in the Classroom represents the application of ideas gained from laboratory experiments to a social problem. Rosenthal was originally interested in how the self-fulfilling prophecy operated in psychological research. More specifically, he wanted to know if experimenters, who had certain expectations about how their subjects should behave, somehow unintentionally transmitted cues to the subjects, which caused them to behave as predicted. Rosenthal conducted a series of experiments to test *his* hypothesis (i.e., that an experimenter's expectancy of how the subject should behave will cause the subject to behave as expected) and most of the results supported the idea of an "experimenter expectancy effect." These findings have caused laboratory psychologists to become more concerned with how they conduct their experiments so as to avoid any experimenter expectancy effect.

More important for our purposes, however, is the fact that Rosenthal became interested in seeing if such a thing as a "teacher expectancy effect" existed and if it could help explain the lowered achievement of ghetto children. Rosenthal first looked at previous research and theory and found much circumstantial evidence to support the proposition that teachers have lower expectations for lower-class and minority-group children's achievements and that the expectation itself then results in lower achievement. We say "circumstantial evidence" because most of the research cited (Rosenthal & Jacobson, 1968, pp. 51–57) simply showed (1) that minority group children fall further behind majority-group children with each passing grade (so it is not just "what they bring with them" that causes the lowered achievement) and (2) that teachers of minority-group children generally don't expect as much of them as they do of middle-class white children. But these studies don't tell us which came first—the expectation or the lowered performance. That is, they don't rule out the possibility that lowered pupil performance *causes* lowered teacher expectancy.

When Rosenthal and Jacobson wished to test their hypothesis they ran into an ethical dilemma: Should a teacher be led to believe that a pupil (who has been randomly selected so that on the average he is no more or less intelligent than others in his class) will soon begin to do poorly in school? In order to test their hypothesis directly they would have to induce such a negative expectation, and then see if pupil performance decreased. They decided that such a study was not ethically justified (since if they were right, some pupils would start performing more poorly through no fault of their own) and instead asked: If a teacher is led to expect that a particular small number of children (again, randomly selected from the class) will show a spurt in intellectual growth in the near future, will these children show an actual upward movement in their intelligence scores?

Rosenthal and Jacobson tested the teacher expectancy effect in the following way. In the spring of 1964 all the children in an elementary school serving a lower-class community were given a disguised measure of intelligence. Purportedly the test measured intellectual "blooming"; that is, it identified those children who "*will* show a more significant inflection or spurt in their learning within the next year or less." In the fall of 1965 teachers were given lists with the names of from one to nine of their children and were told that these were the students who would shortly bloom. In fact, however, these names were drawn randomly from the school list and the children were, on the average, no more or less intelligent than their nonblooming peers. The same intelligence test was administered again later in the academic year. In general, the results at the end of the first year supported the Rosenthal and Jacobson hypothesis: those children identified as bloomers showed a greater gain on the intelligence test than their nonblooming classmates.

Pygmalion in the Classroom has been subjected to much methodological criticism (e.g. Snow, 1969) and some attempts to replicate this study have failed (e.g. Fleming & Anttonen, 1971). The available evidence is suggestive enough,[8] however, for us to ask (1) Does the self-fulfilling prophecy account for some of the *lowered* achievement among ghetto children? (remember: Rosenthal & Jacobson dealt only with expectations for *increased* performance) and (2) if the self-fulfilling prophecy is operative, *how* does it work?

In attempting to answer the first question we must first ask, Do teachers of inner-city school children expect their pupils to perform at a lower level than that of middle-class suburban children? The answer here is an overwhelming Yes. Earlier we mentioned that Becker (1962) found that teachers who remained in ghetto schools tended to lower their academic standards. Over a decade later, a study contrasting one

---

[8] The attempted replications were conducted after publication of *Pygmalion in the Classroom* and the teachers involved may have been attuned to teacher expectancy effects and may have actively worked to overcome them. This is particularly probable in the Fleming & Anttonen study since the teachers were told that the study was concerned with "1. The relationships between the intelligence test information given teachers and the academic performance and self-concepts of their pupils . . ." (p. 5).

group of teachers who were transferring out of slum schools (*leavers*) with a second group of teachers who were not *(stayers)* found that *stayers* adjusted by lowering their academic standards and "increasing their tolerance for pupils' misbehavior and deviation from middle-class standards," while *leavers* maintained their academic standards and even "increased their efforts to maintain strict discipline in the classroom" (Wayson, 1965, p. 230). The same lowered expectations and reduced standards for ghetto children have been expressed by Harlem teachers (Clark, 1967) as well as those in ghetto schools across the country (Coles, 1967).

These studies, however, do not tell us whether the lowered expectancy helps bring about the lowered performance of ghetto children. A good way to study the process is to observe a particular group of children over an extended period of time. Such a design (called a *longitudinal study*) was employed by Ray Rist (1970) who followed a group of ghetto children from the time they entered kindergarten in the fall of 1967 until they finished their third year in public school.

Although no formal intelligence or ability tests were given to the children in kindergarten, their teacher assigned them to one of three tables within eight days after she first met them. The children at the first table, which happened to be closest to the teacher's desk, were labeled by the teacher as *fast learners* while she felt that those at the second and third tables were hopelessly lost in school. That is, without standardized measures of ability or potential and with only eight days of experience with the children (and almost none of this time was devoted to assessing intellectual potential) the teacher grouped the children and saw these groups as reflecting differences in academic promise. (We will put off for awhile discussing the factors on which the groups did differ.) At the end of their kindergarten year the children were given an intelligence test. There were no statistically significant differences among the groups although those at table 1 (the teacher's fast learners) did score slightly higher than the others.

The following year eighteen of the original children ended up in the same first-grade class and were again assigned to groups. The seven children at table 1 in kindergarten ended up in group A (the top group); ten out of the eleven who had been at tables 2 or 3 were assigned to group B (the intermediate group); and one from table 3 went into Group C (the lowest group). Thus, *no one* moved up to the fast learner group, and, although some of those at table 3 moved to the middle group, this was not really a step up, since group C was made up primarily of children who were repeating the first grade. Those who moved up did so only because there were other children in the class who were identified more clearly than they as "failures." The assignment to groups in the first grade was based on "hard facts"—the children in the first group had completed the necessary assignments in kindergarten while the others had not. This makes sense, unless we note that the kindergarten teacher spent more time with these children and in many other ways (to be discussed shortly) helped them to complete their lessons, while this was not true for the other two groups.

The same pattern emerged when the children reached the second grade. On the third day of the term the children were assigned to groups: the highest group, the Tigers, was comprised of all children who made up Group A in the first grade; the middle group, the Cardinals, was made up of students from Groups B and C; while the lowest group, the Clowns, consisted of students repeating the grade and students who were new to the school. By now the self-fulfilling prophecy had already completed itself. The assignment to groups was based primarily on a reading test given at the end of the first grade and scores on the test closely paralleled group assignment. Thus, assignment to particular groups after only eight days of kindergarten and in the absence of data on the children's ability led to "objective" differences in reading performance (and grades as well) by the end of the first grade.

The Rist study illustrates the self-fulfilling prophecy within a particular classroom. There is also evidence that the self-fulfilling prophecy operates when there is grouping on a class level. Such grouping—called *streaming* in Great Britain and *ability grouping* or *tracking* in the United States—is quite common and is based on the assumption that children learn better when they are in a class with children of similar ability. The available evidence indicates that this supposed advantage of grouping does not exist: the most talented students did about the same in ungrouped schools (students randomly assigned to classes) as they did in grouped schools, and in general grouping did not enhance achievement (see Backman & Secord, 1968, pp. 80-83).

Grouping not only fails to improve learning but has a number of distinct defects as well. Placement in a particular group is not based simply on ability. A middle-class child with a particular IQ or ability score is more likely to end up in a high group or track than a lower-class child with the same score. And, "dirty, badly clothed children appear in the lower groups to a considerably greater extent than their test performance warrants" (Backman & Secord, 1968, pp. 80-81). The tragedy of such nonability grouping is that it is relatively permanent. The rate of switching from one group to another is between 1 and 5 percent whereas normal changes in IQ scores should produce a rate between eight and forty times as great! The final link in the chain is objective performance differences: with each year in school, achievement test scores show wider and wider variations among pupils, and the gap is much greater in schools that use grouping.

As the Rist study illustrates, the assignment to groups in early grades is often not based on objective measures of intellectual ability. However, even the use of so-called objective measures (e.g., IQ tests, reading-readiness tests) is questionable in many instances. For example, many IQ measures have a strong verbal or language component and it is foolish to interpret as a lack of intelligence or ability a low score on such a test by a child who speaks Spanish or a black dialect. A more subtle difficulty in interpreting objective test scores arises from differences in how children view the test situation, the test-giver, etc. That is, minority-group children may score low even when their ability is high simply because they are inexperienced in or frightened by test situations (Knowles & Prewitt, 1969, pp. 35-37; Wrightsman, 1972, pp. 207-208).

Yet, despite the lack of objective indicators, assignment to groups is not likely to be random. Indeed, the Rist study shows that socioeconomic status and related variables were highly correlated with group assignment. The children at the "better" tables came from families with higher incomes, their parents had more formal education, and they were more likely to be living with both parents.

The children also differed in (1) their social behavior (those most self-assured in interacting with the teacher ended up in higher groups), (2) their language behavior (those who employed a closer approximation to standard English were placed in higher groups), and (3) their appearance (the cleanest, neatest—i.e., most attractive—again arrived in higher groups). The same extraneous (i.e., nonintellectual) influences on grouping and expectancy show up in other studies. The importance of attractiveness, for example, is demonstrated by a recent experiment by Clifford and Walster (in press). A sample of fifth-grade teachers was given a summary of a student's academic record (showing the student to have received above average grades) and a photograph (half of the teachers got a photograph of a child previously judged to be "attractive" while the other half saw a previously judged "unattractive" photograph). The teachers were then asked to rate the child on a number of scales (remember: all teachers received the same information on the child's grades but for half of them these grades were linked to an attractive child and for the other half to an unattractive child). The teachers rated the attractive child as having a higher IQ, being more likely to have parents interested in education, and going farther in the educational system. Thus, the child's attractiveness led these teachers to infer greater intellectual potential and ability.

Inner-city youngsters, *as a group*, tend to bring to school with them the kinds of external markings (i.e., low socioeconomic status, use of a nonstandard dialect, and what to the teacher is probably an unattractive appearance) that lead many teachers to downgrade their estimates of the children's ability. The question is, HOW is the expectation mediated? How does it influence teacher and pupil behavior in such a way that the pupils actually do learn less and progress more slowly? First, we will look at how the teacher is influenced.

To begin with, teachers of lower-track classes or ghetto schools generally have lower morale and see their job as more demanding and less rewarding than that of their counterparts in the suburbs (Backman & Secord, 1968; Clark, 1967). Although the next step is not certain, the teacher's discouragement probably leads to less animated and enthusiastic classroom presentations, which the children interpret as a lack of interest in them and their progress. Regardless of their enthusiasm level, however, teachers attempt to teach less to students whom they think are not too capable. This was true in the Rist study and is vividly illustrated in two other studies. In the first (Beez, 1970), a group of graduate students enrolled in a teacher training program were asked to help at a Head Start center by teaching a child how to solve as many of a series of puzzles (a symbol learning task) as possible in ten minutes. Half of the "teachers" were informed that their "student" had a "normal" IQ while the other half were led to believe that their student was of "low average" intelligence. (In fact, the two groups of learners were not different on an intelligence measure.) The teachers who thought their students were low average attempted to teach many fewer symbols and spent more time on nonteaching activities.

The same finding held up in a larger study conducted by Ira Goldenberg (unpublished). Observers visited a total of five first-grade classrooms in two different schools on several occasions over a period of three months. On each visit the observer recorded the amount of time the teacher spent with each of the reading groups and the time of day she met with each group. With the exception of one teacher (who spent approximately equal amounts of time with each group) the teachers spent *more* time with the "better" groups than with those ranked lower in terms of potential reading ability. In addition, the "better" groups more often met with the teacher at the times when she was at her best (i.e., the first hour or so in the morning and the period right after lunch). It is informative to note that the teachers said they were allocating their time evenly. They may have been lying, but it is more likely that they simply were unaware that they were "cheating" those children who apparently needed the most help.

The self-fulfilling prophecy is also mediated by the manner in which the teacher interacts with her students. Rubovits and Maehr (1971) found that teachers more often call on students they see as "brighter." In addition, teachers direct their comments more at the "brighter" students. Rist (1970), for example, found that the kindergarten teacher in his study used only that portion of the blackboard which was in front of table 1 (her fast learners), as if she were unaware that the blackboard did, in fact, extend in front of the other two tables as well.

A number of observers of urban schools have noted that teachers and school administrators attribute the lowered achievement of their students to factors *beyond the control of the school*, e.g., lack of intelligence or motivation on the part of the students or the poor quality of their environment. This tendency seems to result from the need to attribute responsibility (or causality) while at the same time seeking to avoid damaging one's own self-esteem. In a laboratory experiment conducted by Johnson et al. (1964), a group of students taking educational psychology courses served as "teachers" for two "students." One of the students did well on both parts of a learning task. For half of the teachers the other student performed poorly on both halves of the task, while for the other half this student did poorly on the first half of the task but much better on the second half. (The performance of both students was preprogrammed and the change in performance was unrelated to the teachers' attempts to teach the students.) At the end of the first half of the task both groups of teachers attributed negative characteristics (e.g., lower IQ, less motivation, less ambition) to the student who did poorly. Thus, they "explained" his poor performance as due to personality traits or intellectual ability which the learner "brought through the door with him." Further, at the end of the second half of the task, those teachers whose students did improve tended to attribute this improvement to what the teacher did while those teachers whose students did not improve said the student was responsible. In sum, the student is perceived as the cause of low achievement and if the teacher's efforts don't bring heightened scores then, again, it is the student's fault. The contributions of the school, the teacher, the methods, and the curriculum are seldom questioned.

Grouping and teacher expectancies also influence the students in such a way as to make the expectancies come true. This occurs in three basic steps. First, the children know what group they are in and what is expected of them. In some cases the teachers don't seem to want to hide this, e.g., in two reported cases the lowest reading groups were called the *Flounders* and the *Clowns*. Second, those in the lower groups tended to turn off school and/or accept the teacher's judgment thereby seeing themselves as "dumb." In a questionnaire study of fifth- and sixth-graders in inner-city schools, Ogletree (1970) found (1) higher absentee rates and a greater expressed desire to stay away from school among those in lower groups, and (2) greater acceptance by those in the lower groups of the statement, "Do you think this is a dumb group?" These points are made clearer by looking at examples of what the children themselves wrote in response to the following two open-ended questions: "How do you feel about being placed in this group?" and "Why were you placed in this group?" Those in the lowest group answered the first question by writing: "I'm dumb." "Please, put me in another class; I don't like it." "This class is bad. I feel so good in another class." They wrote the following to answer the second question: "I don't work hard enough." "I'm not good in books." "Because I hate school." And the final step occurs when the children's lack of interest in school and lack of faith in themselves produce the low performance levels that were expected of them.

The recognition that the self-fulfilling prophecy operates quite powerfully in urban schools leaves us with the problem of how to reduce or stop it. One step seems obvious: stop the practice of rigid ability grouping and substitute flexible, nonability-determined classroom groups. A more important step for inner-city schools is to prepare teachers to be aware of their prejudices and stereotyped beliefs and to provide in-service training to prevent informal school norms from swamping this earlier training. Such training may be quite important: Rosenthal (1966) has some tentative evidence that individuals who are aware of their biases and the self-fulfilling prophecy are less likely to obtain expectancy effects.

Chapter 5

Disorder in the Court System

Americans, both urban and rural, are concerned about "law and order" and they feel that the authorities have not been tough enough in dealing with criminals. In a 1969 poll, George Gallup found that 75 percent of his respondents felt that the courts were not dealing "harshly enough with criminals"; in a 1972 poll 83 percent of his respondents felt that the "police and other law enforcement agencies in the U.S. should be tougher than they are now in dealing with crime and lawlessness" (Gallup, 1969; 1972).

Since most Americans and officials at the highest levels of our national government have linked the alleged increase in crime and breakdown of law and order to the coddling of criminals by judges and others connected with our judicial process, we have chosen to examine the courts in this second chapter dealing with the failure of the city's major institutions.

In addition to the courts, we might have looked at the local political structures, the police, the welfare agencies, or the prisons. All these institutions are in serious trouble and all are factors in producing crime or, more appropriately, in producing criminals. We chose to minimize our examination of these institutions and to look at the courts because we think that concern about law and order and "crime in the streets" is a symbolic issue for many white, middle-class urban and suburban dwellers; the courts, as they perceive them, have become the symbols of what is most frightening about city life. We shall explain what we mean by a symbolic issue later in this chapter; first let us examine the data we have on the courts.

THE NONSYSTEM BREAKS DOWN

Throughout American history two ideal models of the judicial system have competed for major influence in shaping our legal process as it actually exists: (1) the crime control model and (2) the due process model (Packer, 1968).

The crime control model has the reduction or elimination of crime as its goal. In order to work successfully toward this goal, the system must produce a high rate of arrests and convictions in a highly visible, uniform, and efficient manner so that the guilty are punished and future criminal acts by other citizens are deterred. Furthermore, it should not overburden the available resources (financial and intellectual) of the community. Hence the system should include a minimum of ceremonial rituals that might interfere with the speedy and efficient processing of each case. Packer suggested that the appropriate image for such a model would be "an assembly line conveyor belt down which moves an endless stream of cases, never stopping, carrying the cases to workers who stand at fixed stations and who perform on each case as it comes by the small but essential operation that brings it one step closer to being a finished product" (1968, p. 158). At the start of the assembly line stand the police who perform the investigative work and set the case in motion down the conveyor belt. At the other end are the correctional experts and parole boards who either store the product away, make modifications, or judge the product as worthy for release into the society. In between the police and the corrections people is the conveyor belt—the judicial system—manned by a sequence of administrators who perform "a series of routinized operations whose success is gauged primarily by their tendency to pass the case along to a successful conclusion" (Packer, 1968, p. 159).

The due process model, on the other hand, has as its goals the determination of guilt and innocence within a context that guards the civil liberties of the individual against the power of the state. Packer (1968) has suggested the obstacle course as the image for the due process model. "Each of its successive stages is designed to present formidable impediments to carrying the accused any further along in the process" (p. 163). It is a very inefficient model by design. It would cost more to run than the crime control model and it would leave open the possibility that some persons guilty of crime would not be punished. Therefore, in theory at least, it might provide less of a deterrent to future crime.

How does the actual court system compare with these two ideals? The answer depends upon who you ask. The defendants, the police and prosecutors, the judges, defense lawyers, and civil libertarians all have different perspectives and each would give a different description of the judicial system as it presently operates in our urban centers.

If one were to ask the average defendant in a case about his image of the court system, as Jonathan Casper (1972) has done, a very distinct picture emerges. The typical defendant perceives himself as alone in a machine controlled by an all-powerful prosecutor. The judge, the central figure in the due process model, is virtually superfluous in the view of the defendant, who takes his cues almost entirely from the prosecutor. The defendant's attorney is seen as simply a middleman who moves back and forth between prosecutor and defendant with information, and offers and counteroffers. In the case of indigent defendants, the attorney, a public defender, is seen as working for the state just as the prosecutor does. Furthermore, he is not perceived as working very hard in the defendant's behalf in opposing the wishes of the state. When Professor Casper asked one defendant, "Did you have a lawyer when you went to court the next day?" the man replied, "No. I had a public defender" (1972, p. 101). From the defendant's perspective then, the court system clearly resembles the purest form of the crime control conveyor belt.

Others, including some policemen, prosecutors, law and order advocates in the general public, and many politicians, have a different picture of the courts. They see a system in which Supreme Court decisions have so hampered the forces of law enforcement that the power is entirely in the hands of the criminals and their lawyers. Thus, guilty persons go free to commit other criminal acts and justice suffers at the hands of this coalition between the Supreme Court and the criminal elements of our cities. Those who hold this view of the courts look to the crime control model as their ideal and thus feel the courts have failed because they fall so short of this model.

Civil libertarians, many legal scholars, and most appellate justices have yet another image of the court system. They see factors such as poverty and race, which should be irrelevant to the judicial procedure, contributing to a situation in which the state has resources vastly superior to those of most defendants. For the civil libertarians and justices, the ideal model is the due process obstacle course, and the present system falls far short of this norm.

The actual day-to-day behaviors of the courts include elements of all three of the above perceptions. The due process model was written into the United States Constitution and is supposed to influence most of the formal structure of our legal system. On the other hand, the courts allowed the crime control model to guide most actual judicial and police behavior until well into the twentieth century. For example, even though the fourth amendment to the United States Constitution forbids illegal search and seizure (search and seizure without a warrant), the police in many cities were free to conduct such activities until 1961. This is because the courts accepted illegally obtained evidence until the U.S. Supreme Court ruled in the case of Mapp v. Ohio that such evidence was inadmissible in court. To the extent that such evasions of the Constitution are still permitted, the court system does not approximate the due process model.

Nor does the court system appear to be controlling crime very well. It does poorly at deterring first offenses and miserably at deterring subsequent offenses by those who have been down the conveyor belt. In American cities, 40 percent to 67 percent of all those who have been arrested, convicted, and paroled commit a second or a third crime. This is hardly the recidivism rate of an effective deterrent system. Furthermore, the system is anything but efficient at punishing crime already committed. The National Crime Commission estimated that only one-half of all crimes are reported to the police and only one-fourth of all reported crimes result in arrests. Half of the arrests result in dismissal of charges and 90 percent of the other half are cleared by guilty plea while 10 percent result in trials. Thus, less than 1 percent of all crimes result in trials and less than 6 percent are cleared by guilty pleas (cited in Campbell et al., 1969, p. 266).

Moreover, the system is influenced by the supposedly legally irrelevant factors of the wealth, race, education, age, and sex of the defendant. In a study of 1,949 state cases and 981 federal cases, Nagel (1966) found that blacks, the poor, and the uneducated were especially disadvantaged when it came to obtaining bail, a good defense attorney, and a light sentence. The young and females received more informal treatment (treatment that dispensed with pretrial hearings and grand juries). This resulted in lighter sentences for women and youngsters, but it also involved fewer constitutional safeguards to protect their innocence. Nagel suggested that women and juveniles were probably treated in this more informal fashion because of paternalism or patronizing attitudes on the part of the middle-aged males who run the courts. The most important factor in creating the disparity in treatment of all defendants was wealth, which was even more important in determining the likelihood of conviction and the length of sentence than race or sex (Nagel, 1966). We shall return to this factor below.

The most obvious characteristic of the judicial system is that the conveyor belt is on the verge of grinding to a halt. There are simply too many cases for the system to handle, which results in an incredible backlog. Consequently, accused persons must wait a year for a trial in some cities and up to two years in others (Friedman, 1972). Those with money await the trial at home (and some of them will commit crimes to get the money to repay the bail bondsman) and those without sit in jail.

It is the persons in this latter group who really suffer. In the first place, many city jails are jammed to their limits. In New York, the intended capacity of the jails for male prisoners awaiting trial was 2,177, but in August, 1969, those jails were incarcerating 6,484 persons per day (Campbell et al., 1969). Not only are the jails extremely overcrowded, but they also have high rates of homosexual attack, assault, and guard brutality, even higher than those of prisons housing persons already convicted of a crime (Campbell et al., 1969). And finally, 70 percent to 90 percent of all persons in jail are held there only between arrest and trial, and released once a verdict is rendered

(Friedman, 1972). In other words, to get released, one must plead guilty.

HOW DID THIS HAPPEN?

Most experts in the field suggest that this crisis in our cities' judicial system has three roots: (1) a total lack of organization and coordination in the system, (2) overcriminalization, and (3) isolation from other programs concerned with the causes of criminal and antisocial behavior. Let us look at each of them.

Throughout much of this chapter we have been using terms such as *criminal justice system, judicial system,* and *court system* as a shorthand for the interactions and interrelated activities of the police, prosecutors, judges, court administrators, correction officials, jailors, and parole officers. But to use the word *system* in these terms is to imply a degree of order and coordination that simply does not exist. In his chapter for the Violence Commission's Task Force on Law and Law Enforcement Report (Campbell et al., 1969), Daniel Freed describes the chaos that exists in what he terms the "nonsystem of Criminal Justice." Freed is saying that we do not have a system at all in most cities, but a "fragmented and often hostile amalgamation of criminal justice agencies" (1969, p. 268). The police view the courts as the enemy, justices tend to think of the police as violators of the law themselves, and both view the correctional agencies as failures.

According to Freed, there are virtually no formal mechanisms for introducing harmony or at least coordination into the system, and informal mechanisms are rarely utilized. For example, judges, police personnel, and prison officials seldom meet to confer on common problems. Perhaps most importantly, each agency in the nonsystem must compete with every other agency for tax dollars. Consequently, the isolation and antagonism are multiplied rather than reduced. And nothing substantial is being done about this problem.

Therefore, one step toward reducing the backlog of cases and its attendant misery would be to reorganize and coordinate the activities of the various elements of the judicial nonsystem. Psychologists and other social scientists with skills in systems analysis and management could play a very important role in such an organization.

In addition to poor organization, most observers point to overcriminalization as an important factor in overloading the court and criminal justice nonsystems (Dobrovir, 1969; Freed, 1969; Friedman, 1972; Packer, 1968). By *overcriminalization* we mean the use of criminal sanctions (prison and/or severe fines) to regulate behavior that is offensive to a large or powerful segment of the population but not particularly injurious to anyone. William Dobrovir (1969) divides these overcriminalization statutes into three categories: (1) those dealing with morals, such as sexual behavior; (2) those dealing with illness, such as drunkenness or possession of narcotics by addicts; and (3) those dealing with nuisances, such as disorderly conduct, obscenity, and vagrancy.

The conduct or behaviors being regulated by such statutes have common characteristics according to Dobrovir:

... either there is no "victim in the usual sense of the word, because the participants in the offenses are willing; or the defendant himself is the "victim"; or the interest of the victim is often so insubstantial that it does not justify imposition of the criminal sanction to protect it. Therefore, one of the essential reasons for imposing criminal penalties—to deter conduct that is clearly and significantly harmful to the persons or property of others—is lacking (1969, p. 552).

These laws are rarely enforced, or the courts would be even more overloaded than they are. However, when they are enforced it is usually in a highly discriminatory manner. For example, although most states have laws against both prostitution and the frequenting of prostitutes, crackdowns upon prostitution rarely involve arresting the male customers. In the overwhelming majority of cases it is the prostitute who is arrested. Furthermore, the discrimination is frequently along political lines. Although the use of marijuana is quite widespread in many affluent suburbs, it is political radicals and those seeking changes in the drug laws who are most likely to be arrested for possession of pot (Anderson, 1973).

Given the limited resources that our cities and states are willing or able to give to our courts and to law enforcement in general, it seems tragic that so much time and effort should be devoted to attempts at suppressing prostitution, gambling, homosexuality, marijuana smoking, intoxication, and foul language, while crimes such as murder, rape, and assault are being committed in our cities. As we indicated above, the jails of New York City are loaded to the bursting point and the court dockets are months and in some cases years behind; yet, in January, 1973, the time of one courtroom and one judge was completely monopolized during a ten-day trial to decide if a motion picture entitled *Deep Throat* was obscene. [Though the judge ruled that it was, many people in New York, New Jersey, and New England still thought it was worth seeing. The film cost $25,000 to make and grossed over $3.2 million (Blumenthal, 1973).] The trial alone gave the film thousands of dollars worth of free publicity in New York City and kept the show running in Manhattan weeks after such films normally close. Meanwhile, prisoners in the New York City jails awaiting trial were committing suicide or pleading guilty to crimes they had not committed rather than wait any longer for a trial.

Overcriminalization, therefore, is a major factor in overloading the judicial nonsystem. But its effects extend beyond the boundaries of the courts. In addition to draining resources from the effort to control violent crime, it has three important psychological consequences for the public, which may contribute to the general level of criminal behavior in our cities. First, overcriminalization criminalizes behavior regarded as legitimate by substantial segments of the society. The criminalization of this "legitimate" behavior can further isolate or estrange these segments, putting yet another barrier between them and the larger society. Second, being arrested, even for public obscenity or drunkenness, gives a person an arrest record and runs him through the judicial nonsystem in the same way as "real" criminals, murderers, or robbers. A study by Schwartz and Skolnick (1962) has shown that when people know that another person has been arrested, *regardless of the crime or outcome of the case*, they perceive him as a criminal. This makes it difficult for the defendant in an overcriminalization case to get a job and increases his likelihood of conviction in a subsequent court case. Perhaps even worse, having been treated and labeled as a criminal by the society at large, the defendant may come to accept that label and subsequently engage in "real" criminal behavior (Becker, 1963).

A third consequence of overcriminalization is that it invites discriminatory enforcement patterns by the police and courts. In both instances it contributes to disrespect for law and undercuts the end that law is intended to serve.

Another important step, therefore, toward reducing the load on the nonsystem would be to remove the laws creating victimless crimes from our statute books or to reduce them to the level of misdemeanors such as jaywalking or overtime parking. Of course, it is one thing to suggest that these laws be removed and something else to achieve it. The laws against obscenity, drunkenness, and prostitution are important symbols of the government's concern with and reverence for the feelings and values of powerful segments of American society. As we shall see later in this chapter and in Chapters 6 and 7, symbolic issues arouse powerful emotions in people.

In addition to poor organization and overcriminalization, a third major factor contributes to the breakdown of the nonsystem of justice; it is the isolation of the courts from civic and community agencies and programs intended to reduce the breeding grounds of crime: education, job training, medical care, and housing (see Chapters 3 and 4). All too frequently judges, prosecutors, and correction officials behave as if these other programs did not exist or, worse yet, as if the programs were attempting to undercut the task of correction and rehabilitation. Closer ties with welfare agencies, for example, might reduce the need for high bail bonds (or any bail bonds at all—see our discussion of the Vera experiment below) and thus reduce the population of those in jail awaiting trial (Freed, 1969).

MAKING BAIL

In addition to a huge backlog of cases and high rates of recidivism, another consequence of the breakdown of the judicial nonsystem is plea bargaining. Plea bargaining or bargaining for justice is a direct result of the workings of the bail bond system in most American cities.

In the United States, a person arrested and charged with a crime is entitled to be released from detention during the period between his arrest and trial. However, in order to ensure that the defendant will appear at the trial, he must post a bail bond, which is forfeited if he does not appear. Bail bondsmen make their living by posting the bond and charging the defendant a percentage of the bond.

Although bail bondsmen have no official standing with the court such as lawyers or prosecutors have, they are nevertheless very powerful figures in the lives of most defendants. The judge sets the bond, but the bail bondsman can refuse to sell his services to a defendant, and thus leave him in jail, even though the defendant is eligible for bail and has the money to pay for the bondsman's services. Persons of minority races and those associated with unpopular political causes are especially likely to discover this fact of court life (Singer, 1969). Even though the bond is set at the same amount, it may be easier for an accused murderer and rapist to get released than a political radical.

Those most likely to stay in jail during the pretrial period are the poor. The average charge by a bondsman for his services is 10 percent of the bond (Friedman, 1972). Thus, on a $500 bond (the minimum amount in most cities), the charge would be $50, which is a lot of money for a person who is unemployed or one of the working poor.

BARGAINING FOR JUSTICE

The ability to make bail is a crucial asset in plea bargaining, a practice in which the prosecutor negotiates with the defendant for a guilty plea. The court dockets are overloaded and hopelessly backlogged, and, besides, it is very expensive for the state or city to go to trial. Therefore, the prosecutor must attempt to induce as many defendants as possible to plead guilty.

Jonathan Casper has likened this process to a game that has at least two and possibly three "sides." Each side has its own resources and desired outcomes. "The outcome," according to Casper, "depends largely upon the vigor and skill with which each side exploits its resources" (1972, p. 77).

From the perspective of the defendant, the two most obvious sides of the game are the prosecutor and the defendant himself. Sometimes the defendant perceives that the defense attorney has a side of his own and in a few instances, the defense attorney is seen as merely a go-between in the negotiations. Usually, however, the defendant views the attorney as being either on his side or on the prosecutor's. Generally, when the defendant pays for the attorney's services, he perceives the lawyer as being on his side. When the attorney works for the public defender's office, the defendant tends to view his lawyer as working for the prosecutor. There is some real basis for this perception, but much of it rests upon the defendant's assumption that persons drawing money from the same source (the government or the defendant) must be on the same side of the negotiation.

As the game is played, the defendant cannot really win, though he may minimize his losses. (Even if he is acquitted or the charges are dropped, he must pay the bondsman or sit in jail and he may also have to pay for a lawyer.) It is the prosecutor who has the real power because "he's the man who gives the time," as Casper's respondents told him repeatedly (1972). That is, while the judge is the person who is formally and legally responsible for setting the length of a sentence, in practice judges almost always follow the recommendation of the prosecutor and most judges are viewed by defendants as being virtually dispensable. The prosecutor can also dismiss or not prosecute the case; he can reduce the charge (from selling narcotics to simple possession of narcotics, for example); he can drop some charges; and he can give longer or shorter sentences (thus altering the length of time until the convict is eligible for parole).

There are limitations upon the power of the prosecutor, however. He may know that the case against a certain defendant is weak or that the evidence was obtained illegally (and therefore would be of little use in a court battle). He feels pressure to turn over as many cases as possible because jails and court dockets are crowded and a trial takes a great deal of time, effort, and money. Therefore, the prosecutor wants as many defendants as possible to plead guilty and to accept the sentences he offers them.

The defendant has three possible resources: (1) money, (2) status, and (3) fortitude (Casper, 1972). The most valuable of these is money because it can give him status, enables him to hire the best defense attorney, and, most important, purchase his freedom. If he has money, or his friends can raise the money, a defendant can pay the bail himself or get a bondsman to post it, thus securing his release from jail. Once out of detention, the defendant may be able to locate witnesses who will strengthen his case; also, he can continue to work, thus increasing his chances for probation if convicted. If he actually goes to trial, he may be better equipped psychologically to face it than a detained arrestee. Finally, he is obviously in a much better position to hold out against the offers of the prosecutor than if he were jammed into a filthy, violent, and foul-smelling jail.

If he does not have money or status, a defendant needs considerable fortitude, since the only thing he can do is sit in jail and hope that the prosecutor will eventually make him a good offer. As we have already indicated, most arrested persons have little else going for them but fortitude.

The plea bargaining game is played in a series of encounters between the defendant and the prosecutor with the defense attorney taking messages back and forth between them. The prosecutor offers a specific sentence or combination of reduced charges and sentence, and the defendant has the option of accepting or rejecting it. His lawyer may give the defendant some advice based upon his knowledge of how good the case is against the defendant. The defendant knows that, if he goes to trial and is convicted, he can expect a much stiffer sentence than anything he would get by pleading guilty. Hence, 90 percent of the cases that get to the plea bargaining stage are settled by a guilty plea. If he rejects the first offer of the prosecutor, the defendant may get a better offer or he may be told to take it or leave it. When the defendant accepts the offer, a little ritual, called the *cop-out ceremony* by the defendants (and most prosecutors), ensues in which the defendant appears before the judge and swears that he is pleading guilty because he is guilty, not because he made a deal or expects a lighter sentence (Casper, 1972).

The above process is aptly named plea bargaining because it resembles quite closely the bargaining situation discussed by social psychologists John W. Thibaut and Harold H. Kelley in *The Social Psychology of Groups* (1959). The prosecutor has "fate control" over the defendant since, whenever the prosecutor makes a move or an offer, he will affect the fate (in this case the number of years in prison) of the defendant regardless of what the defendant does.[1] The prosecutor attempts to convert this fate control to "behavior control," i.e., control over what the defendant does or how he responds, by communicating his intentions to the defendant through the defense lawyer.

The defendant also has a form of fate control over the prosecutor, but his total power is much less and he only has two potential responses: (1) he can plead guilty or (2) he can hold out for a trail. The

[1] See Thibaut and Kelley (1969), especially Chapters 2, 7, and 10, for formal definitions and discussions of the concepts used here: fate control, behavior control, Comparison Level for alternatives (CL_{alt}) and nonvoluntary relationships.

defendant has this control because, if he demands a trial, the prosecutor's fate is then affected to the extent that he must endure the costs (time, money, effort, etc.) regardless of his wishes in the matter, since this is guaranteed to the defendant by the Constitution. The defendant attempts to convert his fate control over the prosecutor to behavior control (e.g., moving the prosecutor from offering two to five years to offering one to three years) by communicating through the defense lawyer. In the bargaining situations studied by Thibaut and Kelley, a person having a viable alternative to his present situation (in the defendant's case, getting out on bond) had more power and could negotiate a better deal.

It appears that this is exactly what happens in the case of bailed as opposed to detained defendants. In a study of persons arrested for serious crimes in New York City, Foote (1958) found that 53 percent of the bailed defendants, as opposed to 81 percent of the detained defendants, closed their cases by pleading guilty,[2] and 54 percent of bailed defendants received suspended sentences while only 13 percent of the detained defendants were so fortunate. An earlier study conducted by Foote (1954) in Philadelphia yielded similar results: 12 percent of the bailed, as opposed to 48 percent of the detained, defendants eventually were sentenced to prison. Since Foote took pains to show that releasing prisoners on bail was not determined as much by the severity of the crime or their likelihood of appearing in court if released (the criterion by which the decision is supposed to be made according to legal theory) as it was by the ability of the defendant to pay the bondman, it appears that released defendants do indeed have more power. A more sophisticated quantitative analysis of Foote's data (Rankin, 1964) revealed that having been detained during the pretrial period made the defendant forty-seven times more likely than a nondetained person to receive a prison sentence even after background factors such as the defendant's previous record were controlled.

THE VERA STUDY

An even more impressive demonstration of the effects of pretrial detention upon the power of the defendant to achieve a more favorable out-

[2] These calculations were made by the present authors from data reported by Foote (1958).

come of his case was the Manhattan Bail Project of the Vera Foundation (Ares et al., 1963; Freed & Wald, 1964). In this project, a group of law students and other interested volunteers screened all indigent defendants (except certain sex and drug offenders) in the felony courts of Manhattan in 1961. On the basis of factors such as prior record, family ties, and length of residence in New York City, the defendants were designated as good or poor risks for appearing in court if released. The researchers then randomly selected half the good-risk group to be recommended for release on the defendant's own recognizance (that is, released without the need to post a bail bond). This created two groups, both composed of good risks to appear in court and equivalent in all other ways except that the persons in one group had been recommended for release and those in the other had not.

The judges released 59 percent of the recommended group and only 16 percent of the nonrecommended group. (The judges did not know whether or not the persons in the nonrecommended group had been screened and judged bad risks.) *All but a tiny handful of those released appeared in court on the day of their trial.* Even the few who did not appear at the appointed time had not left town. In most cases they had not received the notices of their trial date. Virtually 100 percent of the persons released on their own recognizance eventually appeared in court. In the recommended group (a majority of whom were released during the pretrial period) 60 percent were acquitted or had their charges dropped while this favorable outcome was attained by only 23 percent of the nonrecommended or detained group. Furthermore, persons in the recommended or released group were ten times less likely to receive a jail sentence than those in the nonrecommended or detained group (7 percent versus 73 percent, respectively).[3]

---

[3]One possible explanation for the results of the Vera study is that judges and prosecutors were impressed by the fact that persons in one of the groups had been recommended for release by a panel that had studied their cases. This would indeed weaken the argument that release or detention per se was the factor influencing the outcome; we are not, however, suggesting that this is the only factor. As we indicated above, credibility is an important asset for a defendant. Therefore, a defendant recommended by the panel, whether he was released or not, might have increased his social power by increasing his credibility. Unfortunately, published reports on the Vera project (Ares et al., 1963; Freed & Wald, 1964) do not give us the data necessary to untangle the relative effects of freedom and of credibility resulting from the recommendation.

The overall results of these studies lend strong support to our evaluation of the social power of the detained and released defendants. As Thibaut and Kelley's theory would have predicted, the released defendants had more power to obtain favorable outcomes than did the detained defendants. However, the studies do not rule out the possibility that outcomes are influenced by other social psychological factors in addition to social power.

Perhaps the most important aspect of the Vera study is that its social policy implications are clear: the number of persons held in pretrial detention can be reduced drastically without increasing the risk of defendants not appearing at trial. Those recommended by the Vera group for release on their own recognizance represented a random sample of most defendants and were therefore as likely to "skip town" or to appear in court as any group of defendants. Therefore, releasing virtually all defendants on their own recognizance should not increase the "no show" rate and would at the same time materially reduce the strain on our cities' jail facilities and reduce the excesses of the plea bargaining system.

There has been a great deal of research into the psychology of the courtroom, the jury, and the trial (see Schubert, 1972, for an exhaustive review). However, we shall not go into these studies here because so few criminal cases actually go to trial. Instead, we wish to return to the question of the deep concern about law and order expressed by many Americans.

THE "GREAT CRIME WAVE"

Those who have done research into the judicial nonsystem have found a great deal to be concerned about. The nonsystem is poorly managed, backlogged, and bogged down with overcriminalization. Furthermore, the indigent must spend long periods in jail before coming to trial, the outcomes of the judicial process are biased against the poor and ethnic minorities, and plea bargaining creates a situation where justice, legal safeguards, and the merits of a case are less important than bargaining skills and social power. All these factors can create a situation that breeds disrespect for the law and for society and hence may increase rather than decrease crime. Not one of the social scientific studies, however, found any evidence that the courts were being too lenient. Nevertheless, the public and its most vocal spokes-persons appear to be convinced that this is the case (Gallup, 1972). Therefore, we want to close this chapter on the courts by looking at the nature of America's concern with crime and the breakdown of law and order.

Data on crime are very difficult to gather and assess. The official statistics are notoriously inaccurate. According to a survey of 10,000 representative households by the National Opinion Research Corpora-tion for the President's National Crime Commission, over 50 percent of the crimes committed against citizens were not reported to the police (Campbell et al., 1969). Furthermore, some local police depart-ments inflate their crime rates in order to frighten the citizens into voting more money for the police while others depress their crime rates in order to show what a good job they are doing. Thus, the crime data published by the police not only do not reflect the actual level of crime, but may not even reflect accurately the fluctuations in the level of crime over time.

It is also difficult to make long-term comparisons of national crime rates because these rates are based on the data voluntarily reported to the FBI by local police departments; moreover, the FBI's *Uniform Crime Reports* did not even cover the entire nation until after World War II. Nevertheless, these are the only data we have for the most part and they are revealing in relation to the clamor about rising crime and the breakdown of law and order.

Rates of reported crime have risen over the past decade or so (Friedman. 1972). A little perspective on this rise is necessary, how-ever. If we consider the homicide rate—the crime statistic which is usually the most accurate and the one most likely to be available before 1945—we discover that while this rate was higher in 1970 than in 1960, the 1970 rate was considerably lower than those of 1925, 1930, and 1935.

Crime Level and Concern about Crime

It is significant that the perceived threat from violent crime is not very highly correlated with the level of actual or reported crime. During the years 1965 to 1970, while public concern with crime was approaching its peak, the murder rate was declining.[4] A second example of the exaggerated perception of the level of crime is provided by a recent unpublished study conducted by the authors. In a telephone survey of New Haven residents[5] we found that the median estimate by our respondents of the percentage of households that were victims of a crime in 1972 was 37 percent. On the other hand, only 2.1 percent of them reported having experienced a crime during that year.[6] Clearly, though very few respondents had experienced a crime, most *thought that crime was rampant.* Moreover, while concern with law and order, as measured by items similar to those used by Legant (1972), was unrelated to having experienced a crime, it correlated +.73 with the *estimate* of the percentage of households that had experienced one. That is, concern about law and order was related to high estimates of the crime rate, but neither the concern nor the high estimates were based upon personal experience with crime.

The high level of perceived crime in our sample was probably in part the result of the extensive crime coverage in the local news media. A study done in Colorado, for example, showed that public concern with crime correlated more highly with the level of newspaper coverage of crime than with the level of actual crime as reported by the local police (Davis, 1952).

The Crime Wave as Symbolic Politics

We would suggest, though we cannot prove it here, that the extensive recent media coverage of crime is both a contributing factor to and a reflection of the symbolic nature of the law-and-order issue. By a symbolic issue, we mean a political issue that is based upon a minimum of concrete reality and thus serves as a giant ink blot onto which masses of people can project a number of fears and

---

[4] Though the homicide rates were declining, other, less accurately measured, rates of violent crime were increasing.

[5] To draw a random sample of households with telephones, a series of random four-digit combinations were dialed for each of the New Haven exchange prefixes. This enabled us to compensate for persons who had unlisted phone numbers or who were not in the telephone book for other reasons.

[6] We wish to thank Dr. James Vaupel whose informal survey of his class at Duke University suggested this little study to us. In his class, even though the students were reasonably well informed about crime rates, the estimate of the percentage of families experiencing a crime was 22 percent.

concerns.[7] The issue of law and order, then, has become a symbol onto which fears about many of the changes taking place in American life can be projected. That is, many people have a high level of vague and general fear resulting from rapid social change. They explain and cope with their inner fear and uneasiness by attributing these feelings to the presence of crime or the lack of law and order. By perceiving crime as the source, they externalize the fear and call for crime's reduction as a means of reducing that fear.

The symbolic nature of this issue is perhaps best illustrated by a study of the correlates of voting behavior in the 1969 mayoral election in Los Angeles. In that race, voters perceived Sam Yorty, the incumbent, as being "hard" on the law-and-order issue while they perceived his opponent, a black man named Thomas Bradley (who was, ironically, a retired police captain), as being "soft" on this issue. A survey of a sample of Los Angeles (white) voters revealed, however, that those living near high-crime areas were not more willing to vote for Yorty than those living in objectively safer districts (Sears & Kinder, 1971). What is more important, while the respondents' feelings of personal safety were not correlated with voting for Yorty, the more abstract question, "Do you think women are safe on the streets at night?" did distinguish between Yorty and Bradley supporters. In other words, both Bradley and Yorty voters felt personally safe in the streets and in their neighborhoods, but Yorty supporters (regardless of sex) differed considerably (sixteen percentage points) from Bradley supporters in their feelings about the safety of women in the streets. Thus, supporting the hardline law-and-order candidate was not based upon either objective reality or upon personal fears about one's own safety. Such support was based principally upon fears about abstractions at some distance from the voters' immediate life situation.[8]

---

[7]See Edelman (1971) for a discussion of the nature and uses of symbolic issues in American politics. See Sears & Kinder (1971), Sears & McConahay (1973, especially Chapter 8) and Chapters 6 and 7 of this text for discussions of symbolic issues in race relations.

[8]We are not claiming, however, that concern about law and order was the only factor distinguishing Yorty supporters from those of Bradley. Racism also played a role. However, as Sears & Kinder (1971) demonstrate, it was not old-fashioned racism that distinguished the types of voters. Rather, it was symbolic or abstract racism (see Chapter 7 and Sears & Kinder, 1971). We might add, however, that Bradley took pains to defuse the symbolic law-and-order issue in his 1973 campaign against Yorty by using prominent billboard displays of himself in his policeman's uniform. And he won in 1973, although other factors were involved in his victory.

The possible symbolic nature of the law-and-order concern is further illuminated by examining the other period in this century when law and order was a major political issue. In this inaugural address of 1929, Herbert Hoover enumerated the grave dangers facing the country and then declared:

> The most malign of all these dangers is disregard and disobedience of law. Crime is increasing. Confidence in rigid and speedy justice is decreasing. I am not prepared to believe that this indicates any decay in the moral fiber of the American people (© 1929 by The New York Times Company. Reprinted by permission).

His remedy for this danger sounds familiar: "vigorous police effort," "special tribunals" to deal with court cases more efficiently, changes in the "selection of juries" and reorganization of the police and other investigative agencies so "that justice may be sure and that it may be swift."

Hoover was elected at the close of an era of unprecedented affluence and social change in America. Life-styles, morals, and race relations were undergoing important alterations and it was thus a period of great uncertainty in which economic concerns could be relatively subordinated to symbolic or value issues. Shortly after Hoover's inauguration all of that was changed, however. The stock market crashed and *even though crime rates continued to rise between 1929 and 1933,* Franklin D. Roosevelt made no mention of crime or law and order in his 1933 inaugural address. He stated that "our greatest primary task is to put people back to work" and then outlined a program of economic reform through which he intended to accomplish that task (*The New York Times,* March 5, 1933).

The 1960s and early 1970s were quite similar to the 1920s except that the changes in life-styles, morals, and race relations were even more pronounced in the later period. In this age of affluence and rapid social change we believe people are once again projecting their fears and uncertainties onto the symbol of law and order. As in Hoover's time, in the Nixon era the courts are being blamed for producing a rise in crime by not dealing harshly enough with criminals.

We would concur that the judicial nonsystem needs to be changed and that it may even contribute to crime, but the studies by social scientists have produced no evidence that the courts coddle criminals. Unfortunately, so long as the perception of coddling by the courts and the exaggerated fear of crime persist in the general public, we shall never marshal the resources necessary to produce the needed restructuring of the system.

The symbolic nature of the crime or law-and-order issue will make it very difficult to deal with. Symbolic issues arouse powerful emotions (Edelman, 1971; Sears & McConahay, 1973) and because they have moral and social deference overtones, it is difficult to reach compromises. But we must learn to deal with this very real problem of political psychology. If ever there were an area where research was needed, this is it. Psychologists and others sophisticated in psychological theory and empirical research methodology must find ways to defuse the law-and-order issue as part of our efforts to reform the judicial nonsystem.

Chapter 6

The New Urban Blacks

In the middle 1960s urban whites discovered that blacks, too, lived in their cities. Blacks had been moving into the cities of America, North and South, for over fifty years, but, for most of that time, they were psychologically invisible to Northern whites. Consequently, when blacks began burning and looting property in their ghettoes, whites were taken by surprise and, in some instances, their feelings were hurt because they had believed that the Northern cities did not have a race problem. Unfortunately, those cities did (and do) have a race problem even though Northern whites had ignored it until the bloody events of 1964 to 1969 called it forcefully to their attention.

In the next two chapters we shall examine important aspects of the two sides of urban racial conflict. In this chapter we look at the riots of the 1960s and the social psychology of the most active participants in the riots: the *new urban blacks*. In Chapter 7, we shall examine the social psychology of white perceptions of blacks in general and especially of black militancy.

BLACK INVISIBILITY

For years many blacks felt that they were invisible to whites. In 1947, a gifted black writer, Ralph Ellison, published a novel about growing up black in white America: *The Invisible Man*. After the Los Angeles (or Watts) riot of 1965, young blacks told Martin Luther King, Jr. that they had won the riot despite its heavy toll of death and destruction among blacks because it had made whites pay attention to them (King, 1967, p. 112).

About the time the young blacks were telling Dr. King about their feelings of invisibility, blacks of every age were saying the same thing to survey interviewers from the University of California at Los Angeles. Analyses of these interview responses showed that, throughout the black community, the Watts riot was interpreted as a violent protest to call whites' attention to their mistreatment and neglect of blacks (Sears & Tomlinson, 1968). What may be more important, viewing the riot as an attempt to gain attention was closely related to being optimistic about its results (Sears & McConahay, 1973). That is, those blacks who felt the riot was an attention-getting device also felt that it would produce positive changes. Thus, blacks' feelings of invisibility were related to their interpretations of the riot and their hopes for its eventual impact upon American political and social reality.

Blacks felt invisible, and in a sense were invisible, to whites in the Northern cities. We do not, of course, mean that literally, but rather that, in the perceptual and psychological world of whites, blacks did not occupy any kind of a significant place until after the riots. Blacks lived in one part of American cities and whites in another (Taeuber & Taeuber, 1966). Blacks attended one set of schools (integrated with a few poor whites) while the vast majority of whites attended another set (Coleman et al., 1966). Blacks were rarely mentioned in the major (white) newspapers of the cities before the riots, even during the civil rights era of 1954 to 1964 (Johnson, Sears & McConahay, 1971). And, on the few occasions when blacks and whites did cross paths, the blacks were in a subordinate position to the whites. Those wishing to gain a sense of how invisible the inferior can be rendered in such relationships should try to remember the facial features of the last waiter or waitress (regardless of race) who served them in a restaurant.

As a consequence of their physical and psychological invisibility to whites, blacks were largely politically invisible as well (except on the one day every year or two when the black legions could be turned out to vote for machine candidates). In effect, whenever political and administrative decisions affecting the lives of blacks were made, the politicians and bureaucrats running the school systems, welfare bureaus, police departments, housing agencies, hospitals, and so on, made their decisions either on the basis of what was most convenient for them or on the basis of the anticipated reactions of whites, without regard for the needs of blacks (Jacobs, 1967). This form of institutional racism (Carmichael & Hamilton, 1967) was not deliberately malevolent toward blacks, even though it always worked to their disadvantage. But, in addition, black invisibility may also have fostered deliberate exploitation by allowing the (white) exploiters to dehumanize their (black) victims (Johnson, Sears & McConahay, 1971). Social psychological experiments have shown that the more psychological proximity a potential exploiter or harmdoer feels toward his victim, the less likely he is to exploit or harm him (Milgram, 1965).

WHO RIOTED?

The psychological invisibility of blacks also insulated white urbanites from the reality of the race problem in the Northern cities. Consequently, urban whites were caught by surprise by both the occurrence and the intensity of the riots. After the surprise passed, whites became outraged, vindictive, and fearful (Sears & McConahay, 1973; see also Chapter 7), but they could no longer deny that they had a group of angry blacks in their midst.

Without any knowledge to guide them, white mayors, police chiefs, and ordinary citizens began to create theories about who these newly discovered rioters were. Some said the black rioters were Communists or their dupes; some said they had been incited by TV; others were sure that they were the riff-raff, criminals, and thugs who constituted a small fraction of the ghetto community and who were rejected and repudiated by it. Still others said the rioters were the uneducated and unemployed lower classes. Many whites identified them as the products of broken homes. Every mayor of a riot-torn Northern city announced publicly that the rioters were Southerners newly arrived in their city; some whites even proclaimed that the rioters were all of these things combined.[1]

All these white theories concerning who rioted had three elements in common. *First*, the characteristics attributed to the rioters (Communists, riff-raff, Southerners, uneducated, etc.) by any white official or group always cast the blame for what happened outside their own sphere of influence. *Second*, since the whites who offered these theories regarding who had rioted did not consider themselves responsible, this implied that others would have to make the sacrifices necessary to bring about change. Black criminals would have to be put in jail, Southern whites would have to become more liberal, the school systems should do a better job of educating, and on and on. White officials and white urban dwellers would not be inconvenienced or forced to change. *Third*, the theories as to who rioted were devoid of any manifest political content, as were the solutions implied. If the rioters were those identified by whites, existing power relationships in the cities and across the nation would not be affected by the solutions. More police, more job training, more education were needed, but power and prestige did not need to be redistributed.

Despite the obvious psychological benefits of these theories for whites, most social scientists found little evidence to support them. Survey research following the Los Angeles riot (Murphy & Watson, 1970; Sears & McConahay, 1973) and surveys conducted for the Kerner Commission (NACCD, 1968) following the Newark and Detroit riots revealed that the rioters were no more likely to be uneducated, unemployed, previously arrested, newcomers to the city, and/or products of broken homes than nonrioters. There were only small and inconsistent differences in riot participation between those high in education and those low in education, between the middle and lower classes, between newcomers to and long-term residents of Los Angeles. The rioters certainly were not just a small fraction of the ghetto riff-raff (Sears & McConahay, 1973; Fogelson & Hill, 1968), nor were they re-

---

[1]In writing this chapter, we have relied heavily upon the very extensive analysis of the urban riots of the 1960s, especially the Watts riot, by Sears and McConahay (1973). In order to avoid excessive references to this work, which would distract from the continuity of our presentation, we shall acknowledge our reliance upon it here and then keep all further references to a minimum. For details of the analyses and arguments presented here, see Sears and McConahay (1973).

jected by the overwhelming majority of the nonrioting black residents of the urban ghettoes (Sears & Tomlinson, 1968; Sears & McConahay, 1973). Furthermore, despite diligent efforts on its part, the FBI reported to the Kerner Commission that it found no evidence of any significant Communist involvement in the riots (NACCD, 1968).

If the rioters were not the Southern newcomers, the riff-raff, or the down and out, who were they? Researchers in both Los Angeles and Detroit found that young persons born or reared in the Northern ghettoes where the riots took place were disproportionately represented among the riot participants in those two cities. For example, as shown in Table 6-1, persons between fifteen and twenty-nine who were "native" to Los Angeles were the most likely to have been identified as active participants in that riot. It was found not only that these young, urban-reared blacks had been more active in the riot, but also that they had a distinctive set of political and social attitudes,

Table 6-1 Participation in Los Angeles Riot as a Function of Age and Region or Origin

| | Age | | | |
	15–29	30–44	45	All ages
Percent reporting themselves active				
Natives	37%*	9%	0%	28%
Northern migrants	19	17	17	19
Southern migrants	24	21	15	20
All origins	32%	18%	14%	
Percent high in events witnessed				
Natives	52%	43%	25%	48%
Northern migrants	37	21	17	26
Southern migrants	20	28	21	25
All origins	41%	30%	20%	

Note: "Natives" are those born in Los Angeles or arriving before age 17. The number on which these percentages are based is 586.

*The entry is the proportion active in the riot of those meeting the age and migrancy conditions specified. Thus, 37 percent of young natives reported themselves active; the remaining 63 percent said that they were not.

Source: Sears and McConahay (1973, p. 30).

and aspirations. Thus, social psychologists have proposed that a new type of personality, the new urban black, has emerged in the Northern ghettoes (Caplan, 1970; Sears & McConahay, 1973).

In the sections that follow, we shall first examine the demographic changes of the past century that psychologists have hypothesized as the social origins of the new urban blacks. Then we shall review the social and political attitudes and aspirations that have been suggested as the factors influencing young blacks' participation in the rioting.

DEMOGRAPHIC ORIGINS OF THE NEW URBAN BLACKS

The origins of the new urban blacks have been traced to the dramatic changes in the demographic characteristics of the black population during this century. By demographic characteristics or demographic changes we mean alterations in place of residence, education, and age, the characteristics of a person or a population of persons that are recorded by the Census Bureau.

In 1910, the black population in the United States was rural, agrarian, Southern, mostly illiterate (with some brilliant exceptions), and residentially settled. Today, the grandsons and granddaughters of the blacks of 1910 form a population that is urban, industrial, nationally distributed, better educated, and residentially mobile.

For example, in 1860, 92 percent of all blacks lived in the rural South. As late as 1910, 89 percent still lived in the South (although 21 percent of these lived in Southern cities). By 1966, the percentage of blacks in the South had declined to 55 percent. The urbanization of blacks has been even more dramatic than their Northernization. The percentage of blacks living in urban areas has jumped from 25 percent in 1900 to 73 percent in 1960. This rate has exceeded even that of whites, which went from 42 percent to 70 percent during the same period. Furthermore, in the non-Southern regions of America (Northeast, Northcentral, and West), over 93 percent of blacks are urbanized.

Most important of all, the rate of Northernization was highest during the twenties, thirties, and forties, so that, by 1965, persons born or reared in the ghetto (the natives) were the numerically dominant group among young ghetto residents. For example, in Los Angeles at the time of the riots, 58 percent of residents between fifteen and twenty-nine years of age were native to the city and only thirty percent were Southern-reared. Among persons thirty to forty-four years old, twenty-one percent were natives and sixty-one percent were Southerners. Among the oldest residents—those over forty-five—only 8 percent were natives and seventy-two percent were Southerners.

As the black population was becoming Northern and urban, it was also becoming better educated and youthful. There is still a gap between the level and quality of education available to blacks and that available to whites (see Chapter 4) but it has been reduced. In 1940, whites averaged 4.0 more years of education than blacks, but by 1962 the gap was only 1.5 years. More importantly, the illiteracy rate among young blacks had declined virtually to zero. And, by 1966, the median age of blacks was 21.1 years as compared to 29.1 years for whites.

Thus, in 1965, the black population of the country had become urbanized, better educated, and largely Northernized. It was at the same time young, physically vigorous, and jammed into the deteriorating, industrialized centers of our cities.

These demographic changes set the stage for a new array of social and political attitudes and aspirations among the young, Northern, urban natives who were so prominent in the rioting. Thus, it is important both for an understanding of what happened to race relations between 1964 and 1969 and for a glimpse of what future urban race relations will entail to examine these attitudes and aspirations. For convenience in discussing them, we have divided these social psychological factors into two groups. First, we shall examine the social aspirations and evaluations of the new urban blacks and the resulting despair when these hopes and aspirations were not met. Second, we shall examine the political attitudes of the new urban blacks. As a shorthand, we shall call the first the psychology of hope and despair, and the second the politics of violence.

THE PSYCHOLOGY OF HOPE AND DESPAIR

As we shall see, the psychology of the new urban blacks was characterized by hope and high aspirations coupled with a sense of deprivation and despair. In order to explain the dynamics that produced this configuration, we shall make use of a family of social psychological theories known as social evaluation theory (Pettigrew, 1967). This currently prominent theory hypothesizes that people know about and evaluate their life situations and attainments by comparing their present with their past direct experiences and/or by comparing themselves with salient others (Thibaut & Kelley, 1959). When people are doing better or about as well as they have done in the past, or better or about as well as the people with whom they compare themselves, they are likely to feel happy and satisfied. When they are not doing so well as they have in the past or as others are doing, they are likely to feel unhappy, dissatisfied, and deprived. When they are in this latter state, people usually attempt to do something to change it. Parker and Kleiner (1966) found that some relatively or subjectively deprived urban dwellers distorted reality until they became mentally ill. Bettleheim (1943) reported that many concentration camp prisoners stopped thinking about their past lives or comparing themselves with nonprisoners; as a result, they were happy when they got two slices of bread instead of only one or only one beating instead of two. A similar phenomenon appears to have operated in the case of the new urban blacks. However, instead of distorting reality or altering their comparisons, this group attempted to escape the deprivation state by altering their social and political environments.

From 1900 to about 1960, the Northern ghettoes were constantly innundated by wave after wave of new migrants from the South bringing with them vivid memories of that region's violent repression of blacks. These newcomers had limited aspirations and hopes relative to those of persons who grew to maturity in the North. For example, Sears and McConahay (1973) reported that although about 90 percent of both Northern- and Southern-reared young blacks wanted additional education, 83 percent of those reared in Los Angeles felt they would attain that goal as compared with only 63 percent of the Southern migrants. More importantly, Los Angeles natives were more likely than young Southern migrants to want a job or occupation with higher status and income than the one they currently had. Thus, the new urban blacks had higher aspirations, hopes, and ambitions than the Southerners and were therefore relatively more deprived, since both groups were receiving the same discriminatory treatment at the hands of Northern whites.

The higher aspirations of the new urban blacks, despite their equivalent level of discrimination, can be explained by means of the social evaluation theory that we touched upon above. Southern newcomers experienced a great deal of privation before coming North and, because of the castelike nature of Southern race relations, they limited their comparisons to their own experiences and those of other blacks, the great majority of whom were at least as badly off as they were. The new urban blacks, on the other hand, had not experienced the privations of either their fathers or the newcomers, and were therefore more likely to compare themselves with salient whites (for example, whites who had the same educational attainments) especially since the official ideology of the North held that blacks and whites were free to compete with one another for the good things of life. Thus the Southerners were relatively satisfied, while the new urban blacks, who held higher aspirations and were more optimistic, felt more deprived.

The higher aspirations, optimism, and dissatisfaction of the new urban blacks found by Sears and McConahay in Los Angeles have been documented by postriot surveys in other cities (Caplan, 1970; Campbell & Schuman, 1968). A study by Parker and Kleiner (1966) is especially interesting because their data were gathered in Philadelphia before that city had a major riot. Thus, their results showed that the new urban blacks were characterized by the psychology of hope before the riot, ruling out the possibility that the rioting or postriot responses of whites and the government had created this hope.

As part of their study of the antecedents of mental illness among black ghetto dwellers (Parker & Kleiner, 1966; Kleiner & Parker, 1969), these investigators administered an instrument developed by Cantril (1965) called the Self-Anchoring Striving Scale. In this technique, the interviewer asked each respondent to place himself or herself on a ten-step scale (shown as a ladder) with the best possible life on the top and the worst possible one on the bottom. The respondents were asked where they thought they were on the ladder at that moment and where they would like to be in "a few years." The new urban blacks and the young Southern migrants did not differ very much in where they thought they were currently on the ladder, but the new urban blacks wanted to be much higher in a few years than did the Southern migrants. These higher aspirations of the new urban blacks combined with their current levels of attainment produced a state of relative or subjective deprivation in them similar to the deprivation felt by the new urban blacks in Los Angeles. The psychology of hope and despair, then, both preceded the riot and continued into the postriot era.

THE POLITICS OF VIOLENCE

The social and political attitudes of the new urban blacks contrasted sharply with their personal optimism. While their attitudes toward other blacks were positive, their attitudes toward the political structure and white politicians were strongly negative.

When black respondents in Los Angeles were asked "What do Negroes have that whites don't?" only 44 percent of the entire sample gave an answer that stressed some positive characteristic of blacks. ("Soul" was the most frequently cited positive attribute.) Among the new urban blacks, however, 59 percent gave a positive response, indicating a more positive racial self-image than had prevailed in the past. Young blacks (both natives and Southern migrants) were also significantly less trusting of whites, more likely to be uncomfortable at an interracial party or other social event, and more likely to disapprove of interracial marriages. Thus, the more positive racial self-image of the new urban blacks was coupled with feelings of greater hostility toward whites.

The political attitudes of the new urban blacks clearly mark them as a group apart in the cities of America. Relative to older, less educated, Southern-reared blacks, this group had a more generalized political disaffection. By *generalized political disaffection* we mean the feeling that one is not represented by the political process and that political officials are not to be trusted to look after one's needs. This does not imply a rejection of the basic framework of our democratic system but is intended to "connote feelings somewhere between dislike for a few unresponsive officials and rejection of the political system" (Sears & McConahay, 1973, p. 63).

The new urban blacks were also more negative toward white political officeholders of either liberal or conservative orientation and less likely to trust elected officials of any persuasion. Furthermore, although an increase in the level of education generally reduces political disaffection among whites, it had the opposite effect on new urban blacks (Sears & McConahay, 1973). Whites and blacks with less than a grade school education have about the same levels of political disaffection, but the two races diverge sharply as the educational level increases.

This suggests that the political disaffection of whites and blacks rests upon very different socialization and reality experiences.

The positive correlation between education and disaffection for blacks has a very serious implication for those recommendations by the various riot commissions that called for more education as a means of quelling the rioting (NACCD, 1968; Platt, 1971). Although studies of rioters found no relationship between education and riot participation (Sears & McConahay, 1973; Caplan & Paige, 1968), they showed that generalized political disaffection was strongly related to rioting (Sears & McConahay, 1973). This means that more education, *in the absence of other reforms*, would either have no effect upon the level of urban violence or that it might even increase the level of violence!

Attitudes of the new urban blacks toward the Republican party, the police, the mass media, and the local service agencies (welfare, fire department, garbage collection, etc.) were found to be similar to those of other blacks. But this was because *virtually all* blacks had so many grievances against these institutions that the new urban blacks could not possibly have been more negative.

Yet, the new urban blacks were not indiscriminately "down on" everyone and everything. They shared with other blacks generally favorable attitudes toward black civil rights leaders, black elected officials, and black nationalist organizations. Thus, like their social attitudes, the political attitudes of the new urban blacks were greatly affected by racial considerations: they were negative about or disaffected from (white) system politics and quite positive about black politics and politicians whether they were inside or outside the conventional system.

This does not mean the new urban blacks are alienated in the sense that they are not interested in and do not participate in politics. On the contrary, they are highly politicized, especially when compared with their white age peers, who are generally not very active, despite the few highly visible antiwar activists (see Sears, 1969). Compared to older, less educated, Southern-reared blacks, the new urban blacks were significantly better informed and more sophisticated about politics. They had more exposure to the mass media and more experience with unconventional political actions (demonstrations, boycotts, and, of course, riots), but less involvement with conventional politics (as measured by lower voting rates and fewer political contacts).

The picture of the new urban blacks that emerges from these data is of a highly sophisticated and politicized group (although its politicization is in the direction of unconventional American politics). Indeed, when asked about their preferences for future black political strategies, the new urban blacks were more likely than other blacks to prefer demonstrations and violence to the more conventional activities of voting, individual striving, and standard bureaucratic procedures.

As in the case of the psychology of hope and despair, Sears and McConahay (1973) traced the origins of the politics of violence to the demographic changes of the past century. The central part of their thesis was that age peers had a greater influence upon political socialization in the Northern cities than in the rural South. In the densely populated cities young blacks interacted more with one another than with their parents in discussing the dramatic political and social events of the day (the Supreme Court decisions, the civil rights marches, the battles over desegregation, the martyrdom of civil rights workers, etc.); the emergence of peer norms and attitudes was thus facilitated. In contrast, persons growing up in the rural South had less opportunity to interact with peers, and were more dependent upon adults to interpret events for them; hence, peer norms and attitudes were less likely to emerge. Thus, the older generation had less influence upon the political socialization process in the Northern cities than it did in the South. This meant that the attitudes acquired by the young natives were different from those acquired by young persons who had received their socialization before moving into a Northern city.

The content of the socialization was altered not only by the relatively greater influence of peer groups but also by the political and social differences between the two regions of the country. In the North (during the 1940s and 1950s, at any rate), the formal ideology held that blacks were equal to whites rather than being members of a legally and formally defined lower caste. Thus, young Northern blacks had more opportunity to express the hostility resulting from their oppression than did Southerners. This meant that their basic orientation was to move either "against" or "away from the oppressor" rather than "toward" him (Pettigrew, 1964).

The differences in formal practices and ideology between North and South also made possible the development of greater self-esteem and racial pride in the North since the constant reminders of racial inferiority (separate restrooms, eating facilities, bus seating arrangements, etc.) were not present. And, finally, the differences in formal ideology encouraged greater political participation and sophistication (Milbrath, 1965).

Once these processes were set in motion by the differences in formal ideology, they combined with the relatively greater influence of peers who had no direct experience with Southern socialization to accelerate the trend. Thus, by the mid- and late-1950s, the Northern natives, the new urban blacks, were receiving a socialization quite different from both that of the older generations in the ghetto and that of their peers who grew up in the South and moved to Northern cities only after the age of seventeen. These socialization differences were reflected in the political attitudes that Sears and McConahay (1973) and Caplan (1970) found in new urban blacks who had reached adulthood by 1965.

VIOLENCE AS A MEANS OF GRIEVANCE REDRESS

In the years preceding the riots, the new urban blacks reached physical maturity in sufficient numbers to dominate the younger generation (those under thirty) in the ghetto. This—combined with one other factor—created a tinderbox situation needing only a spark to set it off. In one case the spark was provided by an ordinary drunk-driving arrest (Los Angeles), in another by a raid on an after-hours tavern (Detroit), and in a third by an assassination (Washington, D.C.). Regardless of what set them off, however, the conditions leading to the riots were present in every city.

The other factor hypothesized to have produced conditions conducive to riots was the unredressed grievances held by many blacks, young and old, Northern- and Southern-reared, educated and uneducated. These grievances grew out of the discrimination that blacks had experienced at the hands of local officials, local merchants, and the police. They were unredressed because whites were indifferent to the grievances of blacks (who were mostly invisible to them). Hence, blacks perceived that the normal channels for grievance redress were blocked.

The particulars of the grievances differed from city to city, but they almost always involved discrimination in jobs and housing, poor city services (garbage collection, for example), exploitation of blacks by ghetto merchants (through overcharging, unfair credit practices, inferior goods, and quick repossession of goods), and, above all, psychological and physical brutality by the police (see NACCD, 1968; Beardwood, 1968; Campbell & Schuman, 1968; Sears & McConahay, 1973).

The intensity with which an individual felt these grievances largely determined his or her participation in the Watts riot regardless of age or previous socialization. Furthermore, those who were most aggrieved were also most likely to perceive that the grievance redress mechanisms that local politics, individual striving, or administrative review normally provide were blocked to them. Thus, the rioting served as the functional equivalent of politics as a grievance redress mechanism; the riots were the politics of violence. Consistent with this view of the rioting as a grievance redress mechanism is the fact that those we have characterized as new urban blacks were more likely to have been involved in the riots than other blacks. The relatively deprived, the politically disaffected, those with greater black pride, and those who perceived that elected officials were not working for them were all more likely to have rioted than those without grievances and discontents (Sears & McConahay, 1973).

In summary, then, it appears that the demographic changes in the black American population fostered social psychological changes that produced the new urban blacks, and that it was they who led the way in the rioting of the 1960s. Since demographic changes are not likely to be reversed, the new urban blacks will not go away. Furthermore, since whites have not acted very vigorously to unblock the grievance redress channels, our cities will continue to be faced with the threat of racial conflict into the near future, at the very least.

NEW STRATEGIES

All the forces that produced the violent clashes of the recent past are still present in our cities today and an additional element has now been added: the fact that the riots occurred. The riots were a watershed event in the history of American race relations, ending one era and ushering in another. As a result, whites now perceive blacks as more threatening and frightening than they did in the past, and blacks have the example of the riots to use for future political development and future racial and political socialization. We shall take up the new white perceptions in detail in the next chapter. We wish to conclude this chapter by examining potential conflict strategies that the new urban blacks have adopted or may adopt.

First, there is some evidence that the riots aided the new urban blacks and their intellectual leaders in developing a new political ideology. The Los Angeles riots generated much of this ideology spontaneously at the grass-roots level as blacks, participants and nonparticipants alike, attempted to understand and explain to one another what had happened (Sears & McConahay, 1973). In talking about the event, people were able to identify with one another, to begin to articulate their grievances (invisibility, discrimination, exploitation, police brutality), and to explain the riot as a purposeful protest intended to redress those grievances (Sears & Tomlinson, 1968; Sears & McConahay, 1973). With the aid of some very articulate black leaders (e.g., Carmichael & Hamilton, 1967), the folk ideology spread from city to city and took on the characteristics of a more formal ideology: (1) it explained events, (2) it articulated grievances, and (3) it served as a guide for political action. Thus, the riots and the folk ideology they generated served to shape the more structured ideology of Black Power.

Second, the example of the riots may be used by the new urban blacks in socializing a younger generation and resocializing their Southern age peers in the direction of increasing self-esteem, black pride, political sophistication, and politicization (Sears & McConahay, 1973). Individual stories of heroic young black freedom fighters "liberating goods from the man" have made the rounds of the ghettoes after every riot, and the riots collectively have been cited as a time when blacks "got it together" to take effective action. These examples can serve to develop the esteem and identity of blacks much as other stories (about Moses and Pharaoh, for example) developed the esteem and identity of other ethnic groups.

Third, there will be more violence. However, the new urban blacks probably will not resort (unless in desperation) to the mass riots characteristic of the 1960s. The psychological benefits of these riots offset their terrible cost to blacks for a while; however, there are now few additional psychological benefits to be gained, and, furthermore, the police and guardsmen are now armed to the teeth with antipersonnel weapons. Many blacks perceive that large-scale riots would result in an intolerable death toll among blacks (Sears & McConahay, 1973). Instead of this type of riot, we will see a continuation of the guerilla-type attacks upon police and other white agents in the ghetto that began in 1970.

However, violence will be only one of many techniques that will be tried. Already blacks have used many novel and ingenious strategies: sit-ins, bus boycotts, protest marches, demands for reparation, quotas for admission to the white opportunity structure, kidnapping of dignitaries, demands for membership on corporate boards of directors and university committees, strikes, tutoring, studying, legal action, formation of caucuses, and symbolic acts. Some of these have failed, such as the attempted violent escape from the courtroom in San Rafael, California, which resulted in the deaths of many of the defendants and the judge, and led to the trial in which Angela Davis was acquitted of conspiracy. Other strategies have been relatively successful, for example, the attempts to open up universities and scholarly societies to blacks. The range and ingenuity of the techniques used in the past fifteen years have added an entirely new dimension to political activities in America, and we can expect great creativity and flexibility in the years ahead.

Fourth, despite their considerable political disaffection, the new urban blacks will not abandon conventional political activities such as voting, petitioning, and working for candidates. As Burnham (1970) has shown, blacks of all generations are voting increasingly selectively and *en bloc* for both black candidates and white candidates who are strong supporters of blacks' material and symbolic interests. The new urban blacks will, however, show considerably more enthusiasm for black candidates who express a little disaffection than for either moderates who are dedicated to "the system" or radicals who do not share the new urban blacks' optimism.

In addition to electoral politics, future strategies will include negotiations with white politicians, officials, and leaders in which representatives of the new urban blacks either imply or express directly the threat of future violence. This is another of the flexible strategies we can expect (and have seen already), but it is a two-edged sword: while posturing and threatening will satisfy some of the symbolic needs of the new urban blacks, it will also frighten and stiffen the resistance of whites (see Chapter 7).

SYMBOLIC POLITICS

This brings us to what we feel is the most important aspect of urban racial politics: its symbolic nature.[2] As Edelman (1971) has pointed out, politics is only partially involved with the distribution of tangible benefits. Symbols and abstract values are also important elements; in fact, they were a more important element in the climate that produced the riots and in the postriot polarization of the races than more tangible, materialistic factors of immediate self-interest.

A few examples from the data of Sears and McConahay (1973) will illustrate our point. The data indicated that blacks' most vivid grievances concerned white authorities' and agencies' mistreatment of blacks as a group, rather than their own personal situations. Some respondents said they had been victims of police brutality, but a more common complaint was that many blacks in the area had been victimized by the police. Some reported suffering from racial discrimination, but much more common was the complaint that blacks generally were discriminated against. When asked, "What are your biggest gripes or complaints about living here?" many respondents had no complaints and relatively few cited their own economic situations. Deficiencies in personal status were not crucial to the development of disaffection and rioting. In fact, the most disaffected were actually the *best* educated and thus those most likely to profit from the status quo. Similarly, the strongest correlates of riot participation were collective grievances and symbolic racial attitudes, and not measures of personal status. Indeed, Sears and McConahay did not find a single measure of personal status that was significantly related to riot participation.

The new urban blacks were and are especially sensitive to symbolic politics. Though reared in considerably more advantaged circumstances, both economically and politically, than the older Southern migrants,

[2] The case for the symbolic nature of urban racial politics, and the relative importance of issues dealing with concrete, tangible benefits compared with more abstract, symbolic issues in motivating riot participation among blacks (Sears & McConahay, 1973) and antiblack voting among whites (Sears & Kinder, 1971) have been presented in detail elsewhere. Therefore, we shall not attempt to recapitulate those arguments here. They rest for the most part upon a series of empirical findings that show decreasing relationships between issues and political behavior (rioting, voting) as the issues become more concrete, specific, and in the immediate self-interest of the respondent. Here, we wish only to illustrate some of the findings and draw out some of the implications of symbolic politics.

and considerably more optimistic about their own *personal* prospects, they felt more deprived economically, and were more disaffected politically, as well as more likely to become involved in the rioting and to advocate violence. Their discontents were not focused upon concrete, practical grievances; in fact, their most dominant attitudes were a sense of generalized political disaffection and black pride. Thus, the new urban blacks perceived themselves as being involved in a symbolic and collective struggle, one that did not *simply* grow out of deficiencies relating to their own personal material self-interest. As we shall see in the next chapter's discussion of symbolic racism and perceived threat, whites have similar self-perceptions.

Most social scientists, including most psychologists, as well as men of practical affairs, concentrate their efforts upon understanding and attempting to change what they think of as the more "real" economic and materialistic bases of racial conflict, with only a nod to these symbolic conflicts of values. Nevertheless, we think that recent research into racial conflict shows that symbolic conflicts are among the most important ones we must deal with in our cities today. They are the conflicts most likely to lead to insurrection and violence and they are certainly the least susceptible to compromises.

We must hasten to add, however, that we are not saying that tangible self-interest is not involved or that such issues are unimportant. They most certainly are important, although not as crucial, relatively, as symbolic politics at this time. Similarly, we are not implying that economic, social, and structural reforms should be avoided by cynically manipulating symbols (see Chapter 3). White lower-class Southerners, for example, have been the victims of symbol manipulation intended to mask economic exploitation for too long. As Dollard (1937) pointed out, Southern elites played upon the racial fears of lower-class whites in order to distract them from their economic self-interest. Very few blacks would want that sort of "resolution" of the conflict.

We are urging psychologists to devote more effort to the study of symbolic issues (see Chapter 8) so that these problems can be tackled as effectively as the economic problems. And we are warning that any Administration which adopts a strategy toward blacks of "don't listen to what we say, but watch what we do," will find that much of what it does is unsuccessful so long as what it says satisfies the symbolic needs of whites only.

Chapter 7

Things Are Moving
Too Fast

One of the questions commonly asked in public opinion polls on race relations is:"As far as all the things that have been going on lately with Negro rights, do you think things are moving about right these days, too fast, or too slow?" Since the early 1960s large majorities of white Americans have said that things are moving *too fast*. In 1963, for example, 64 percent of a national sample of white adults endorsed the idea that "things are moving too fast" in black-white relations, in a 1966 poll 70 percent concurred, and in the early 1970s these attitudes remain unchanged.

The feeling that blacks are advancing too fast is generally accompanied by negative feelings and beliefs about blacks. The negative feelings and beliefs, however, are not the same ones that predominated twenty or thirty years ago. In fact, there has been a significant decline in the percentage of whites who endorse traditional antiblack stereotypes (e.g., "Blacks are inherently less intelligent than whites"). In this chapter we will discuss two concepts—symbolic racism (Sears & Kinder,

1971) and perceived racial threat (Ashmore & Butsch, 1972)—that are designed to throw light on current feelings and beliefs of whites regarding blacks. We will explain how and why traditional stereotypes have changed, while symbolic racism and perceived racial threat have emerged as important new elements.

THEN AND NOW

Psychologists, particularly social psychologists, have long been interested in the problems of intergroup hostility and conflict. Since Bogardus' pioneering studies of social distance in the 1920s, most psychological research on race relations has focused on the measurement and explanation of racial or ethnic prejudice. "Prejudice is a negative attitude toward a socially defined group and toward any person perceived to be a member of that group" (Ashmore, 1970, p. 253). That is, prejudice is a predisposition to think ill of and respond negatively toward a group, or a person who appears to be a member of that group. Psychologists are interested in intergroup attitudes because these attitudes are seen as predictive of behavior. Psychologists do not argue that attitudes are the sole determinant of behavior toward the attitude-object, but only that attitudes, in conjunction with situational factors (e.g., the norms of behavior in a particular situation), account for overt behavior.[1]

Negative intergroup attitudes are accompanied by *negative feelings toward* and *derogatory beliefs about* the group in question. Over the past forty years, and particularly in the last decade, there have been radical changes in the feelings and beliefs (stereotypes) that whites have regarding blacks.

Katz and Braly (1933) conducted the first major study of stereotypes by asking Princeton college students to select from a list of trait adjectives (e.g., honest, aggressive, unreliable) those that they felt characterized a number of national and ethnic groups (e.g., Negroes, Chinese, Jews). The traits most often ascribed to Negroes were as follows: superstitious (84 percent of the subjects), lazy (75 percent),

---

[1]See Collins (1970, pp. 79–87) for an in-depth, easily readable discussion of the attitude-behavior relationship.

happy-go-lucky (38 percent), ignorant (38 percent), musical (26 percent), ostentatious (26 percent), very religious (24 percent), stupid (22 percent), physically dirty (17 percent), naive (14 percent), slovenly (13 percent), and unreliable (12 percent). Negroes, then, were perceived as primitive or childlike, as passive rather than active, and certainly not as threatening. (This latter point is underlined when we note that "Americans" were seen—among other things—as industrious, ambitious, and aggressive, as were Jews, who were also seen as grasping.) The Katz and Braly study was repeated at Princeton in 1951 by Gilbert and again in 1969 (Karlins et al., 1969). The most striking finding of these later studies was the decrease in subjects ascribing the above-mentioned traditional stereotypes to Negroes. This is certainly due in part to the belief among many college students that it is not socially desirable to stereotype ethnic groups. In addition, however, changes in black-white relations have made the traditional, paternalistic attitudes of whites less relevant. Among whites in general there has also been a marked decline in such stereotypes as stupid-unintelligent, unambitious, smelly, immoral, careless, and so on (Harris, 1971; Schwartz, 1967, particularly pp. 19-22).

This reduction in traditional antiblack stereotypes has not, however, resulted in a reduction of antiblack prejudice. Instead, new beliefs that support white hostility toward blacks and black progress have emerged. Some whites, particularly those living near inner-city ghettoes, now see blacks as threatening and violent. In general, whites living in suburban neighborhoods do not feel directly threatened by blacks. Nevertheless, the turbulent 1960s have induced a general feeling of anxiety that, together with certain traditional American values (e.g., that people should get ahead on their own without government help), has resulted in antiblack attitudes organized around symbolic issues (e.g., welfare). Later in this chapter we will discuss these beliefs in depth, but first we will seek to explain why the changes discussed above have occurred.

Prejudice as a Group-level Phenomenon

There is considerable evidence that the nature of relations between social groups shapes the attitudes of members of each group, i.e., that "the character of the existing relations between ingroup and outgroup generates attitudes toward the outgroup that are consonant with these relationships" (Secord & Backman, 1964, p. 413). In the simplest terms, a positive relationship between ingroup and outgroup (such as working together for some common goal) produces positive attitudes or liking while a negative relationship yields negative attitudes.

Pierre van den Berghe (1967), in a study of race relations in four countries, found two major stages in negative black-white relations: paternalistic and competitive. In the United States the paternalistic stage lasted from about 1661 (with the passage of the first formal slave law in Virginia) to 1865 (the end of the Civil War). During this stage whites regarded blacks as childlike (i.e., intellectually and morally inferior to whites), a view that was quite congruent with the dominant-subordinate nature of black-white relations.[2]

Van den Berghe saw the formal end of slavery as ushering in a new stage—that of intergroup competition. Such a period of competition did occur in many Southern states, with a concomitant rise in the view that blacks were powerful and threatening. Several factors combined to make this a period of short duration. Union troops were withdrawn from the South (the "Compromise of 1877" called for troops remaining in three Southern states to leave). In addition, "legal" (e.g., poll taxes and other Jim Crow laws), quasi-legal (e.g., economic pressure by white tenants on black share croppers), and illegal (e.g., lynchings and threats by the Ku Klux Klan) measures were taken that eliminated black-white competition.

Thus, from about 1890 or 1900 on, blacks were in theory in competition for jobs, housing, etc., but in practice this competition was completely defused so that blacks were not seen by most whites as a direct threat to their economic, political, or social position.[3] The lack of real competition was reflected in white images of blacks. As we saw above, the stereotypes of blacks held by whites in the 1930s and 1940s varied in only minor ways from the perception of blacks as childlike that characterized the paternalistic stage.

[2] There were, of course, times when this image was drastically altered. Slave revolts (see Aptheker, 1969, for a complete discussion) in particular led to the view, for a short time and in a limited area, that blacks were strong and violent.

[3] Again, however, there were periodic, local exceptions to this generalization. The violent reactions of whites to such threats are discussed by Jones (1972, pp. 16–19).

Although Marcus Garvey and some other black leaders of this period proposed "radical" solutions to problems of black Americans (e.g., return to Africa, promotion of a tribal African image) the dominant adaptation on the part of blacks was to withdraw from contact with whites as much as possible, thereby avoiding pain and humiliation. In the 1950s and 1960s the strategy of prominent black leaders shifted to a demand for equal rights (see Paige, 1970, for a fuller treatment of this topic). This grew into the civil rights movement, epitomized by Dr. Martin Luther King, Jr. King's goal of racial equality and integration and his method of nonviolent resistance dominated intergroup relations in the late 1950s and early 1960s, and the civil rights movement produced a number of political victories for blacks (e.g., the Civil Rights Act of 1964).

But by 1965 the civil rights movement was on the wane—some say it was dead (Pinkney, 1969)—and more militant strategies and tactics were being advocated. The summers of 1963 through 1967 saw several hundred urban riots or revolts (see Chapter 6). The slogan "Black Power" was proclaimed and many black leaders questioned both the goals and the methods of the earlier civil rights movement. Although there have been only a few major urban disturbances since 1967, current black-white relations can best be described as in a state of cease-fire rather than of peace. Blacks demand (not ask for) equal power and participation in decision making (not the right to eat at a lunch counter with whites) and whites resist.

To understand this resistance we turn now to the variables of perceived racial threat and symbolic racism. The arguments presented in the following pages should be regarded as informed speculation rather than fact, since we will be covering rather new ideas, which have not been subjected to a large number of tests by independent investigators. We present these new and somewhat unproven ideas in the hope that they will be useful in understanding the present and predicting the future course of intergroup relations.

Perceived Racial Threat

During the paternalistic stage of intergroup relations blacks were seen as childlike (ignorant, carefree, pleasure-loving), but as we move toward more open intergroup competition this image is changing. Many white

Americans are coming to see blacks not as childlike but as powerful and threatening. As we shall see, this image is most pronounced among those most directly in competition with blacks—mainly lower-middle-class whites living in the outer rings of our cities. It is our contention that perceived racial threat contributes to the retreat of these whites from the city to the suburbs and, to some extent, underlies their resistance to scatter-site housing, busing, and related issues.

Perceived racial threat is a type of prejudice, i.e., it involves a negative attitude toward a socially defined group. Unlike antiblack prejudice as traditionally conceived of and measured, perceived threat stresses: (1) the fear component (i.e., blacks arouse the emotion of fear rather than disgust or contempt) and (2) the belief that blacks are actively taking things away from, hurting, or displacing whites.

The first question to be asked is: Does such a generalized fear-threat syndrome exist? Although no systematic, nationwide data are available, several small-scale studies suggest that a rather unitary perceived-threat construct does exist. Groves and Rossi (1970) queried a sample of urban policemen about the extent to which they agreed with the statement "Negroes have tried to move too fast in gaining what they feel to be equality." They were also asked how disturbed they were at "Negroes draining resources through welfare payments," "Negroes taking over political power," "Negroes moving into areas that, until recently, were occupied only by whites," and "Negroes socializing with whites." The responses to these five items were all significantly inter-correlated (i.e., policemen who agreed with the general statement that Negroes were moving too fast also tended to be more disturbed by Negroes on the four specific questions and a high disturbance rating on any specific item went along with a high rating on all the other items). Using different items, a similar perceived-threat syndrome has been found among middle-class high school students and among college students attending a summer school session (Ashmore & Butsch, 1972; Ashmore et al., 1972). In both studies, respondents who felt threatened by blacks in one area (e.g., jobs) also tended to feel threatened in other areas (e.g., housing, education, personal safety). Table 7-1 presents the intercorrelations of six perceived-racial-threat items in the summer school study, which involved almost 1,000 respondents of somewhat diverse backgrounds (some were regular college students; others were part-time students attempting to get a college degree while raising a

Table 7-1 Intercorrelations of Perceived-Threat Items

	Item	2	3	4	5	6
				Item Number		
1	As far as all the things that have been going on lately with Negro rights, things are moving too fast.	.45	.53	.37	.49	.28
2	I would be worried about Blacks moving into my neighborhood because property values would fall.		.42	.35	.38	.23
3	White communities are being shortchanged since such a large percentage of domestic spending is being devoted to Blacks.			.48	.50	.32
4	"Black Power" means Blacks taking from whites.				.51	.30
5	Unless law and order is maintained Blacks will soon be rioting in white neighborhoods.					.28
6	If you were applying for a job and there was a Black applicant for the job, it is very likely that he would be given preferential treatment.					

Source: Ashmore and Butsch (1972). *N*=972.

family). Again, the responses to the various fear-threat questions were significantly intercorrelated, supporting the idea of a perceived-racial-threat syndrome.

The above data suggest the existence of perceived racial threat[4]; it now remains to be seen how perceived racial threat varies from one group to another and how it influences perception and behavior. Although it is our belief that perceived racial threat is on the rise among

[4] The fear component of perceived racial threat is not yet well documented. However, people who agree with perceived-racial-threat items relating to education also tend to agree with items about Negroes being a threat to their personal safety. Also, whites who have been induced to aggress against blacks expect more retaliation than those who have aggressed against whites (Donnerstein, et al., 1972). And finally, while a sample of college subjects did not see blacks as more lazy, bad, or unattractive than whites, they did feel blacks were more unforgiving (Perlman & Oskamp, 1971, p. 508).

most whites,[5] the highest rates of fear-threat can be expected to occur among those groups who are actually in conflict with blacks for jobs, housing, and so on. Although no nationwide data have been collected specifically to test this idea, there is suggestive positive evidence from a number of sources. Campbell (1971) asked whites living in various parts of the United States (1) how they felt about contact with blacks in various settings, (2) how much racial discrimination against blacks existed, (3) how they felt about antidiscrimination laws, and (4) how much sympathy they had for various forms of protest by blacks. On the first three variables there were few consistent differences between those whites living in cities (and hence in greatest competition with blacks) and those living in suburbs. However, on "sympathy with black protest," which can be regarded as a type of perceived-racial-threat measure, place of residence did make a difference: whites living in cities had less sympathy for black protest. In other words, whites most in competition with blacks differed from their suburban counterparts only on questions that appear to tap the fear-threat syndrome we call perceived racial threat.

Correlational data indicate that perceived threat may have a number of effects on perception and behavior. Groves and Rossi (1970) found a significant correlation between perceived threat and the tendency of police officers to view ghetto residents as hostile. This may represent a case of what Allport (1958) calls "complementary projection" wherein a person attributes a certain trait to another person or group in order to "explain" his own emotional state. In this case, policemen who feel threatened may attribute hostility to the community as a way of explaining their own feelings. The possibility that the policemen who scored high on the measure of perceived racial threat were projecting their own feelings is supported by the fact that there was little difference in the amount of perceived hostility found in several different cities even though these cities were deliberately selected on the basis of wide variations in actual ghetto hostility toward the police.

There is also suggestive evidence that perceived racial threat affects the behavior of other members of white society. Caprio (1972) inter-

[5]Greeley and Sheatsley (1971), for example, found that between 1963 and 1971 the feeling that "Negroes shouldn't push themselves where they're not wanted" increased for whites of all ages, places of residence, incomes, and religions.

viewed white residents (many of whom were "working class, second-generation ethnic-Americans") of an inner suburb bordering on a large Eastern city. This suburb had experienced a large influx (200 percent increase) of blacks during the 1960s. Although the residents were generally satisfied with their homes, Caprio noted ". . . a growing lack of commitment to the area." One of the major factors in this growing disaffection was a fear of crime, not from residents of the local community but from youths living in the nearby city (which had a very large black population). That these whites were afraid of black crime is further supported by the fact that those moving from this area were more likely than whites of similar means but living in different neighborhoods to move to "white" suburbs—they were moving away from blacks. Not only were the whites escaping from blacks, but their lack of commitment to the neighborhood also made them unwilling to keep up the maintenance on their houses—"no owner was willing to make any costly repairs (i.e., more than $250). Few, in fact, were willing to make even the most minor repairs" (Caprio, 1972, p. 18). The "social obsolescence" of these houses sets the stage for their rapid physical deterioration ("physical obsolescence"). The oft-heard "When Negroes move in, the neighborhood . . ." may in large part reflect processes set in motion by white residents several years before blacks actually move in.

Perceived racial threat may also be involved in decisions by whites to arm themselves. In 1968, a national sample of adults was asked if they felt they had to be prepared to defend their homes against crime or violence or whether that should be left to the police (Feagin, 1970). About 50 percent of the whites felt they should be prepared to defend their homes. Those who felt this way differed from those who did not on many questions relevant to race. In particular, the "defend homes" respondents were much more likely than the "leave to police" respondents to feel that the urban riots were "a way for black people to take over the cities." That perceived racial threat is related to "home defense" is further supported by data from interviews with whites following the 1965 Watts riot. Morris and Jeffries (1970) found that those most fearful of black threats to their personal safety were most likely to consider buying and using firearms.

Perceived threat is also correlated with how whites interpret the term Black Power and how they perceive harm-doing in biracial settings. Black Power is probably one of the most widely known and emotionally charged slogans of the late 1960s. It was first pronounced publicly by Stokely Carmichael in 1966 and has since received much attention in the mass media. As with any slogan, however, this public exposure has not led to any consensus about what the term "really means." In fact, there are deep differences in the interpretation of the term, differences that help us to understand how competitive intergroup relations are reflected at the level of individual psychological processes.

In the fall of 1967, Aberbach and Walker (1970a) asked a random sample of Detroit-area adults to define the term Black Power. Although there was a wide variety of definitions, these could be reduced to seven general categories. The proportion of each type of response for both blacks and whites is given in Table 7-2. Blacks and whites diverged considerably in their interpretations. Whites overwhelmingly saw Black Power as something that threatened them (38.6 percent of the responses fell in the category "blacks rule whites"). This tendency of many whites to see Black Power as a means of gaining domination over whites is particularly interesting in view of two facts: (a) Blacks in general do not feel this way and (b) media coverage, though stressing interracial conflict, also notes that the vast majority of blacks are striving for equality and not domination (see Mendelsohn, 1970, p. 758, footnote 11).

This suggests that whites' perception of Black Power is shaped by more than what blacks say about the term. A recent study of middle-class high school student (Ashmore et al., 1972) suggests that perceived racial threat may figure in this shaping process. As in the Aberbach and Walker study, the students were asked to define Black Power in their own words. In addition, they filled out an attitude questionnaire that contained several items designed to measure perceived racial threat. Those students with high scores on perceived racial threat were also most negative toward the term Black Power. Nine of seventeen students scoring highest on perceived racial threat gave "unfavorable" definitions of Black Power. It is particularly noteworthy that four of the five "specific" negative definitions fell into the "blacks rule whites" category. On the other hand, only one of the eighteen low-perceived-threat respondents provided such a definition of Black Power.

Just as perceived racial threat influences how whites interpret a slogan such as Black Power, so, too, it affects their perception of

Table 7-2   Black Power Interpretations, by Race

(Question: What do the words "black power" mean to you?)

Interpretation	Blacks	Whites
Unfavorable		
Blacks rule whites	8.5%	38.6%
Racism	3.9	7.3
Trouble, rioting, civil disorder	4.1	11.9
"Nothing"	22.3	5.3
Negative imprecise comments (ridicule, obscenity, abhorrence)	6.5	11.7
Other	4.3	5.9
	49.6	80.7
Favorable		
Fair share for black people	19.6	5.1
Racial (black) unity	22.6	5.6
	42.2	10.7
Don't know, can't say	8.2	8.6
	100%	100%
	(*N*=461)	(*N*=394)

"Other" responses were scattered and inconsistent, although generally negative. They include references to black power as communism, radicalism, a return
to segregation, and a sophisticated failure to define the concept because of a perception that it has contradictory meanings. The latter answer was given by one
black and five white respondents.
Source: Aberbach and Walker (1970a, p. 370).

behavior in an interracial setting. Ashmore and Butsch (1972) gave a
test designed to measure perceived threat to almost 1,000 students
attending a college summer school. A sample of those scoring very low
on perceived threat and a sample scoring moderately high[6] were then
asked to participate in a study of how people learn from newspapers.
The subjects read five newspaper stories and answered questions about

[6] The scale ran from 0 (indicating complete disagreement with six perceived-
threat items) to 120 (indicating complete agreement with all six items). The
low-perceived-threat subjects had an average score of 9; the moderate-perceived-
threat subjects averaged 59. Among the students studied there were only a handful who scored high on perceived threat. It can be expected that higher scores
would be obtained from those more directly threatened by blacks.

each one. The third story concerned an incident in which one man physically harmed another. There were four different versions of this story: a white aggressed against a white, a white against a Negro, a Negro against a white, and a Negro against a Negro. The subject's perceived-racial-threat level significantly influenced how the aggressive act was perceived. (Remember: The act was exactly the same in all cases; the only thing that varied was the race of the aggressor and that of the victim.) Subjects who scored moderately high in perceived racial threat rated the act and the agressor (regardless of his race) more negatively when the victim was white, while the low-perceived-threat subjects were more critical when the victim was black. Thus, even though the act was objectively the same in all cases, those subjects who scored higher in perceived threat were much harsher when the victim was white than when the victim was black.

Low-perceived-threat subjects were also influenced by the race of the actors in the story—specifically, they were harsher when a Negro was victimized. One likely explanation is that these subjects were bending over backward to avoid being racist.

The perceived-racial-threat syndrome is often accompanied by the belief that blacks are receiving special privileges and getting more attention from government agencies than whites. There is no doubt that many governmental agencies are making special efforts to reach blacks and other minorities, and that many companies and unions (often because of government and/or minority-group pressure) are taking steps to overcome previous discriminatory hiring and recruiting practices. On the other hand, discrimination against blacks in housing (Taeuber, 1965; Johnson, Porter & Mateljan, 1971), employment (Duncan, 1968), and other areas continues to put them at a considerable disadvantage vis-à-vis whites.

The reality of continuing discrimination, however, is less important for our purposes than how whites perceive the situation. Several national and local polls show that whites do not see discrimination as a significant block to progress by blacks (e.g., Campbell, 1971). Furthermore, a significant minority of whites feel that in fact it is they who are being discriminated against (see Aberbach & Walker, 1970*b*, footnote 43). The size and tenor of this minority are indicated by the fact that in a sample of Detroit-area adults interviewed in 1968, 46 percent ". . . believed that if they were black they would be either making advances toward their goals in life or advancing more rapidly toward their goal" (Aberbach & Walker, 1970b, p. 1210).

In the preceding section we noted how perceived racial threat among white residents in an inner suburb contributed to both the social obsolescence of their homes and their desire to leave (Caprio, 1972). Perceived inequity was also a factor in these outcomes. Specifically, many white homeowners felt that blacks were given preferential treatment by "lending institutions, real estate brokers, and government." The residents went even further: they felt that these public and private agencies were actively carrying out a policy of *intersection* as opposed to one of *convergence*. Most of the whites recognized that ghetto blacks had a lower standard of living than they did and favored actions to bring the blacks up to the level they occupied (i.e., a convergence policy). However, they felt that government officials and business leaders were instead following an intersection policy, i.e., a policy that would enable blacks in the near future to overtake the inner-suburb whites and achieve a higher standard of living.

The above studies suggest that many whites feel that blacks are getting a better than "fair shake." It is impossible to know how widespread this belief is at present, but it is easy to see how this perceived inequity can combine with other aspects of perceived racial threat to yield a very strong resistance by whites to all forms of progress by blacks. Perceived inequity is an especially important ingredient because it provides whites with a socially acceptable "reason" to oppose particular projects (e.g., busing), particular political candidates, and so on. That is, the belief that "we are being discriminated against" provides a strong justification for actions that may be caused by some vague sense of fear or dissatisfaction. Consequently it seems clear that research aimed at identifying the sources of perceived inequity is of great importance.

Symbolic Racism

While perceived racial threat (and the often-accompanying perceived inequity) helps us to understand some of the resistance to changes in the present race relations status quo (particularly resistance by those most directly in competition with blacks), it is necessary to look at another factor in order to see why the suburban dweller also resists the progress of black Americans. Sears and Kinder (1971) present data that suggest that this resistance stems from *symbolic racism*—a combination of sociopolitical conservatism with a feeling that blacks are attempting to destroy the way American society is organized and run. Symbolic racism does not stem from specific issues of black-white confrontation or from personal threats of blacks to whites; rather it is organized around a set of highly abstract, or symbolic issues.[8] Whites high in symbolic racism have generally grown up with almost no personal contact with blacks and little contact through the media (see our discussion of black invisibility in Chapter 6). They also have been socialized to favor the present socioeconomic status quo. In the 1960s blacks challenged this status quo and symbolic racism was born.

During the Los Angeles mayoralty campaign of 1969 Sears and Kinder obtained interviews from a sample of white suburbanites. This campaign offered a good opportunity to test both the effects of symbolic racism and the value of traditional prejudice measures since it pitted Tom Bradley, a black liberal, against Sam Yorty, the conservative white incumbent. Sears and Kinder found that traditional prejudice measures did not explain voting behavior. They encountered a low rate of acceptance of traditional antiblack stereotypes and much rejection of outright discrimination; and moreover, traditional measures did not predict pro-Yorty feelings. On the other hand they found a high level of symbolic racism[9], which was strongly correlated with pro-Yorty sentiment, even when nonracial liberalism–conservatism was statistically controlled. The Sears and Kinder findings—though they must be regarded as quite tentative since only one sample was involved—suggest that antiblack sentiment among white suburbanites may be focused around

[8]It is important to keep in mind that some whites can be ranked high both in perceived racial threat and symbolic racism and that a high level of both factors exists among white Americans. We discuss the two factors separately because we feel that one can better explain resistance to blacks for one particular subgroup of whites, while the other can explain it better for another subgroup, i.e., perceived racial threat is more significant than symbolic racism among lower-income whites while symbolic racism plays a greater role among whites who are better off socially and economically.

[9]This was assessed by such items as "Streets aren't safe these days without a policeman around" and "Do you think that most Negroes who receive welfare could get along without it if they tried, or do you think they really need this help?" These items don't tap *personal* fears but rather two symbolic issues (crime in the streets and welfare) that are at the center of current black-white relations.

symbolic issues rather than stemming from direct personal fears or traditional stereotypes. That is, for suburban whites antiblack prejudice may be predicated on feelings that blacks are challenging the American way of life and the symbols of that way of life.

WHAT CAN BE DONE?

What can be done to reduce antiblack prejudice (whether based on perceived racial threat or symbolic racism)? To answer this question we must first understand how negative intergroup attitudes are acquired. As we saw above, negative intergroup attitudes develop in a society in which groups are negatively interdependent. Negative intergroup interdependence sets the stage for prejudice; but how is prejudice perpetuated through time? Individuals acquire prejudice in the same way that they acquire other attitudes and beliefs—through interaction with their environment, particularly with other people.

The process of indoctrinating a child into his or her culture is called *socialization;* it involves teaching the child a particular language, a particular way of dressing, a particular set of food preferences, and so on. It also entails teaching the child about "good guys" and "bad buys." In the United States, blacks and other minorities have long been regarded as bad guys, so most majority-group Americans have been socialized into a pattern of antiblack prejudice. Parts of this pattern of socialization are obvious. White parents, for example, often have definite rules forbidding their children to play with blacks and the child is punished for breaking these rules (see Ashmore, 1970, pp. 283-284).

Most socialization of prejudice, however, is more indirect than this, and is often done unconsciously by the socializing agent. Schools rarely teach the facts of race and racial differences. The same situation obtains in the home; as most parents are not acquainted with scientific research on race they tend to respond to children's questions by avoiding them. Some use derogatory stereotypes, but more often parents become nervous and change the subject when questions of skin color, etc., arise (e.g., Goodman, 1964). Such responses teach the child only that blacks are strange, somehow fearful people.

The most subtle, yet potent, perpetuator of prejudice is the process of "putting two and two together" (Ashmore, 1970, pp. 286-288). The stage is set for this process to operate by institutional racism

(Carmichael & Hamilton, 1967). Institutional racism refers to the fact that our political and economic institutions are so constructed that certain groups—particularly minorities and the poor—are doomed to inferior positions. For example, blacks attend the poorest schools in America (see Chapter 4) and then are refused jobs because they don't have the proper educational credentials. Furthermore, they are discriminated against in employment through culturally biased "tests" or restrictive apprenticeship rules so that only the most menial jobs are generally available to them.

The upshot of the current set of institutional arrangements is that blacks and certain other minorities do, in fact, occupy in disproportionate numbers the bottom rungs of the social ladder, holding low-paying and low-prestige jobs, living in inferior and ugly housing, and so on. As we noted in Chapter 3, this state of affairs leads the majority-group Americans to conclude that blacks (and other poor people) *are* inferior. The objective "facts" of blacks' low position in society together with the high value Americans place on self-reliance lead majority-group Americans via the attribution process to the "obvious" conclusion that blacks are inferior beings. Recall that this is the same attributional error that is committed when the poor are regarded as the cause of poverty (see Chapter 3).

Howard Schuman (1969) has recently shed further light on this attributional error. As we noted above, the belief that whites are inherently superior to blacks has been declining for many years. Yet blacks continue to have inferior housing, jobs, etc., and this is recognized by whites. Most social scientists believe that environmental factors (particularly discrimination) account for the blacks' situation, and they have marshaled much evidence to support this belief. In a survey of whites living in fifteen major cities, however, environmental causes were seen as much less important than "something about Negroes themselves." That is, the white public rejects both the traditional racist view that blacks are inherently inferior and the social science view that black-white differences in jobs, etc., are due to discrimination and other environmental factors. Most whites attributed the low socioeconomic position of blacks to something best labeled *lack of motivation*. For example, one respondent said, "They have the same advantages the whites have but they don't use them. They quit work." The Schuman finding is analogous to the point made in Chapter

3 about attitudes toward the poor. In both cases, a group's inferior position needs to be explained (i.e., human behavior is seen as willful or caused) and the American core value of self-reliance means that internal or personal causes are more likely to be chosen than environmental causes. (It is also likely that whites choose internal causes because it frees them from responsibility for the inferior position of blacks.)

This analysis suggests two major ways of decreasing antiblack prejudice: alter the socialization process and end institutional racism. Ending institutional racism and freeing blacks from low-paying jobs, inferior housing, etc. (see suggestions in Chapter 3 on alleviating poverty), would make it less likely that whites would put two and two together and conclude that blacks are inferior beings. The specifics for ending institutional racism revolve primarily around political and legal questions that it would not be appropriate to cover here; however, in Chapter 8 we will point out how psychologists can be helpful in promoting such change.

We can, however, be much more specific in discussing how current socialization processes could be altered to reduce prejudice. Schools are a major socialization vehicle in our society, and at present they do more to heighten racial conflict than to reduce it since the curriculum generally presents a biased view of the role of minorities in the past and present. Moreover, most schools fail to teach "facts" about race and racial differences.

First, what do schools teach about the concept of race? At best, most teachers fall back on empty moralization when questions regarding racial differentiation arise. Take the following question, for example: "Why do they (or, we) have black skin?" Instead of discussing the existence of racial differences, the large degree of overlap between racial groups, the probable evolutionary adaptiveness of racial markers or traits, teachers tend to brush off the question by saying something like "We are all brothers under the skin." This response (while it does seem to exclude one sex from our species) conveys an admirable moral stance, but does not help pupils at all to understand the biological and anthropological facts of race. In the absence of such facts, pupils trained in our schools have no understanding of the concept of race, and perceived racial differences are used to rationalize the status quo: "*They* are inherently lazy or stupid. It is *their* racial heritage."

Schools don't teach about race because it is a "touchy" issue and most teachers assume that children—especially those in the lower grades —are not emotionally capable of dealing with such issues. But race is a touchy issue in part *because* schools don't teach about it. There is no doubt that race is a difficult topic to teach (and at many points the teacher will simply have to say, "That is still an unsolved problem"), but there are many things we do know that would help dispel some racist myths. Richard A. Goldby's book, *Race and Races* (1971), which is written in clear and nontechnical language, covers much of this knowledge and it could be used by teachers to develop their own curriculum on race. The basic point we want to make is that schools should meet touchy issues such as race head-on rather than simply moralizing about them or ignoring them.

Not only do schools help perpetuate racist myths by failing to confront the question of race, but they also present a view of America and the world that often ignores and sometimes derogates the role of minority groups. As we have seen, the mass media, books, and movies have been and continue to be perpetuators of prejudice among majority-group Americans. In the past, this role was obvious since minorities only appeared in stereotyped roles; for instance, as late as 1962, blacks appeared on television almost exclusively in the roles of athletes, entertainers, or servants (Colle, 1967). Today the bias of newspapers and other culture mediators is less obvious since they tend to ignore minorities except when these minorities protest. (There are, of course, many exceptions to this generalization and hopefully the media will one day represent all types of Americans accurately.) This clearly produces a view of minorities, particularly blacks, as pushing and threatening and, as we have seen, such a stereotype is increasingly accepted by white Americans.

The school textbook treatment of minorities has paralleled their coverage by the mass media. In studies conducted in 1949 and 1960, for example, black Americans were generally ignored in textbooks, and when they did appear, they were most often pictured ". . . as slaves and bewildered freed men . . . thus perpetuating the stereotype of a child-like, inferior group of people" (Kane, 1970, p. 77). In a 1969 study of forty-five of the most widely used junior and senior high school social studies texts it was found that the picture had improved somewhat. Blacks were more often mentioned than in 1960 and most of the stereotyped passages were gone. One glaring weakness remained, however. Most texts had no discussion of the African heritage of black Americans (even though the European heritage of most white Americans was quite fully described). This omission contributes to intergroup conflict by alienating, depressing, and increasingly angering black Americans and by perpetuating the myth among whites that blacks were saved from the jungle by white slave merchants ("I mean, they were just running around in their loin clothes all day, weren't they?"). Most texts also continue to do an inadequate job of covering other minorities: (1) the positive contributions of Jews to America are ignored; (2) there is little discussion of American Indians in the present; and (3) Oriental and Spanish-speaking Americans continue to be largely ignored.

Schools can become part of the solution rather than continuing to be part of the problem if the past and present of the various groups making up this country and this world are recognized (in textbooks, bulletin board displays, etc.) and if readers used by elementary school students are "desegregated."

For example, Lichter and Johnson (1969) have shown that readers that portray the pluralistic nature of America can make a difference in children's intergroup attitudes. These researchers conducted a field experiment in which one group of middle-class white second-graders used a multiethnic reader (i.e., one that contained illustrations of blacks, Orientals, etc., as well as whites) while a comparable group used a reader that was identical except that it had illustrations of whites only. Before the experiment the groups did not differ in the degree of antiblack prejudice as measured by four different techniques. After just four months of using the two different readers, however, there was a significant reduction of prejudice for those students using the multi-ethnic reader while no such change occurred in those who had used the white version of the reader. Thus, very small changes in curriculum and texts promise significant changes in student beliefs and attitudes. Such changes by themselves, however, are not enough. Large and continuing reductions in antiblack prejudice will only be effected when the relationships between blacks and whites are altered. In the next chapter we will discuss the role of psychologists in facilitating these changes.

Chapter 8

Where Do We Go from Here?

What ultimately can we as psychologists or students of psychology say or do about our cities' problems of crowding and pollution, poverty, inadequate schools, nonsystems of criminal justice, and racial hatred and violence? In this final chapter, we want to address ourselves to this question in a general way. In the preceding chapters, we have proposed, outlined, and discussed many specific solutions to specific problems. Most of these solutions were more obviously political, economic, or sociological than psychological, and we may have given our readers the impression that, despite our academic credentials and departmental affiliations, we are really not psychologists at heart. Worse yet, we may have created the impression that psychology cannot really contribute to the solution of urban dilemmas.

Neither of these impressions is true; we feel strongly that psychology has a role in and a contribution to make to the process of solving our cities' problems. Unfortunately, psychologists are just now beginning to study urban dilemmas seriously. Therefore, while most of the political, economic, and sociological studies we reported had psychological implications, little of the research was manifestly psychological except in the realms of intergroup relations and schools.

In order to spur and possibly to guide future psychological research in urban problems, we will discuss in this chapter the potential contributions of psychology to this task. We feel that the contribution of psychology can be made through at least three channels: (1) the application of the knowledge of psychology by anyone who acquires it, (2) the actions of individual professionals in the field of psychology, and (3) the activities of the psychological profession, i.e., the lobbying and educational activities of the local, state, and national organizations such as the American Psychological Association. Consequently we are addressing a broad audience in this last chapter.

As the foregoing implies our suggestions are aimed at individual psychologists and at the profession as a whole, in addition to students. Some division of labor among these three audiences may be required to bring about solutions to our urban dilemmas, but we shall be deliberately vague about which of our audiences should follow which suggestion. This is because we want the responsibility for seeking solutions to be shared by everyone. Therefore, each of our readers, regardless of his or her current role as student, layman, or professional, should consider that virtually every suggestion is aimed directly at him or her.

As a way of organizing our suggestions, we shall look briefly at three stages in the process of problem solution: the analysis of the problem, the choice of best or preferred solutions, and the implementation of the solutions. Finally, we shall examine another area in which psychology can make an important contribution: the development of "civics" or "American government" educational curricula that would foster an atmosphere in which debate and conflict over the definition of social problems and their solutions could be dealt with in an open and "civil" fashion. By a *civil* fashion, we mean a process in which individuals and groups in our society would recognize the rights of others to seek social changes consistent with their interests and values and without endangering society as a whole. Labor and management have come to approach this civil fashion of dealing with their conflicts in recent years through the process of collective bargaining. Before this accommodation was reached, neither side acknowledged the right of the other to seek changes and conflict was dealt with in an "uncivil" (and usually violent) fashion involving the massacre of workers and the bombing and destruction of plants and equipment. As a result, this sort of conflict was frequently more costly to both sides than any of the proposed solutions might have been.

WHAT IS THE PROBLEM?

Before any one of our urban dilemmas can be treated as a "social problem," it must be recognized as such. As Ross and Staines (1972) have pointed out, not every problem encountered by individuals or groups in our society is defined as a social problem. Many human difficulties are viewed as individual problems that should concern only those who most obviously suffer from them rather than as social problems to be dealt with by society and the government. Furthermore, once something is perceived as a social problem either by the public, the media, the government, social scientists, or other vocal and/or powerful segments of the society, there still remains the question of just how the problem is defined.

These two aspects of problem analysis, recognition and definition, are well illustrated by the history of poverty as a social problem. For years, poverty in this country was seen and defined as an individual problem resulting from wickedness, sloth, stupidity, or imprudence on the part of the poor. Those correlates of poverty that were perceived by the public as social problems, for example, escape behavior via drugs and alcohol, were recognized as such only because they were perceived and defined by the middle class as threats to their values and well-being (e.g., drinking caused crime and destroyed stable middle-class families). Only when the middle class suffered economic deprivation during the Great Depression of 1929 to 1940 did poverty become a social problem. Today, although members of the middle class acknowledge poverty (somewhat grudgingly) as a social problem, they see it as a problem that society should deal with by using its resources to eliminate the presumed negative characteristics (present-time orientation, for example) and bad behaviors (high illegitimacy rates, for example) of the victims of poverty (see Chapter 3; and also Ross & Staines, 1972; Ryan, 1971; Caplan & Nelson, 1973).

In order for psychologists or students of psychology to make a meaningful contribution to the analysis of urban dilemmas, we must be careful to avoid two very significant pitfalls: (1) the tendency to recognize or be interested in resolving only problems of concern to the middle, upper, and/or managerial classes of society, and (2) the almost irresistible temptation to define the problems that are perceived in ways that readily lend themselves to *"blaming people in difficult situations for their own predicament"* (Caplan & Nelson, 1973, p. 202).

The first of these pitfalls is related to the position of most psychologists in the American social class structure and the sources of funds for psychological research. The overwhelming majority of psychologists and students of psychology either were reared in middle-class families or acquired some important middle-class values in the process of their education. Furthermore, as students, academicians, scientists, consultants, and clinicians we find ourselves in a social position in which our interests and concerns are much more attuned to those of the middle class and above than to those of the working and lower classes. Thus, no matter how often or how forcefully we may reject middle-class values and morality, we tend to have middle- and upper-middle-class perceptions of reality, particularly social reality.[1]

In addition, we are almost always dependent either on the upper classes or on government and business managers for funds to support our research. The price for such support is usually that psychologists (and other social scientists) must study problems recognized and defined by persons in the upper and/or managerial classes. Hence, as Caplan and Nelson (1973) suggested, we study underachievement among the poor but ignore the exaggerated profit motives of certain business executives.

Virtually all social scientists are inclined toward the first pitfall and psychologists, in particular, are susceptible to the second. As we indicated in Chapter 1, our expertise is concentrated for the most part in the science of individual human behavior. Therefore, the temptation to define social problems in terms of individuals is almost irresistible. Once we define a problem in this way, we are dangerously close to attributing its cause to individuals rather than to the system. In Chapter 6, for example, much of the analysis of rioting was in terms of the feelings

---

[1]We must hasten to add that the majority of psychologists are also *white* and *male,* which may explain why, for example, illegitimacy is often perceived as a problem related to the dilemmas of poverty and race relations, while abortion reform, divorce law reform, and the need for comprehensive child care programs are less likely to be seen in that way.

and attitudes of the new urban blacks involved; nevertheless, the cause of the rioting was attributed to a combination of new attitudes and a political structure that blocked the conventional channels of grievance redress open to other citizens in America. We are not saying that causal attributions to persons rather than to systems or situations is always to be avoided, only that attributions to persons can easily lead to inaccurate analysis and to blaming the victim. Moreover, in the case of psychologists, the combination of our place in society and our scientific interests and expertise is one that makes the blaming of individuals a highly probable outcome of our definition of a problem.

The first step in avoiding these pitfalls in problem recognition and definition is to be aware of their existence. The second is to use the theoretical and methodological tools of psychology to examine *all* the psychological dimensions of problem definition. Whenever vocal groups in our cities demand that a social problem be recognized, and defined in a certain way, we should ask why these groups (regardless of their status or power in our society) perceive a certain set of situations and behaviors to be a problem.

When we study a group of persons whose behaviors are perceived by other groups in our society as the cause of a social problem, it is important that we keep in mind a major finding of attribution theory research: Observers often tend to attribute the actions and behaviors of actors to something internal to the actor, some motivational or dispositional factor, while the actors themselves tend to attribute their behaviors to something external, some situational or system factor (Nisbett, et al., 1972). This means that when we are studying the emotions, feelings, perceptions, and behaviors of persons who differ from us, whether in race, sex, values, or economic status, we are much more likely to be fulfilling the role of a "pure" observer; however, when we are studying persons similar to ourselves, we are likely to be both observers and actors. Consequently, we must be especially careful to guard against attributional errors and be highly critical of person attributions in the first of these situations. Person attributions should be made only after very careful observations and after considering other alternative attributions. In addition, we must be careful not to treat real cultural differences between a target group and the majority of the population as deficits to be eradicated in the target group. For example, as we saw in Chapter 4, many urban teachers regard black dialects as deficient forms of standard English rather than as valid language systems. Baratz and Baratz (1970) have shown that such misperception also occurs among social scientists researching social problems.

A third contribution that psychology can make to the process of problem analysis is to compare the actual feelings and behaviors of people involved with the myths about their feelings and behaviors. In some cases this may dispel the myths, in others it may highlight real differences between groups. In Chapter 3, for instance, we saw that the urban poor are quite similar to their more affluent counterparts in some important attitudes (e.g., the work ethic and the value placed on marriage) yet very different in others (e.g., sense of personal power).

Finally, whether we dispel myths or clarify differences or both, as psychologists we can make an important contribution to the process of problem analysis by calling attention to the feelings and concerns of those involved, so that psychological factors as well as economic and political ones may be considered by planners and decision makers. For example, Caplan and Nelson (1973) note that the design, placement, and construction of public housing are almost always based upon political, economic, and technical considerations with little concern for the interests and feelings of those who are supposed to live there. Frequently, the planners and decision makers do not care what the tenants feel until the latter complain; more often, it is a case of tenant or consumer invisibility (see Chapter 6 for a discussion of black invisibility), that is, those doing the planning know very little about the feelings and wishes of the poor. As a result, the wishes of the taxpayers and of the powerful have a much greater impact on them. To counteract this to some extent, psychologists should consult systematically with the prospective tenants of a public housing project (by means of surveys, interviews, or direct observation) and call their feelings and needs to the attention of the planners. To assist in this particular task of building humane public (and private) housing, Ward et al. (1972) have begun to assemble what knowledge we already have of the psychological factors involved in the housing needs of various groups and have published it in a place where it will come to the attention of some planners; however, more work of this sort is clearly needed.

Of course, we are not suggesting that research by psychologists should substitute for direct representation of public housing tenants on planning boards. The two activities—research and representation—are

complementary, not interchangeable. Psychologists and other professionals should always consult and make joint plans with those they wish
to help whether in the realm of public housing, community mental
health, higher education, or in other areas.

WHAT DO WE DO?

We have dwelt at length upon both the pitfalls that face psychologists
and the potential contributions they can make to the definition and
analysis of urban social problems because this analysis implies a best or
preferred solution to the problem. Frequently (and not surprisingly),
the solution implied by the analysis serves the interests of the person or
group doing the analysis. For example, when Northern mayors and
police chiefs blamed the outbreak of urban violence upon Southern
newcomers to their cities (see Chapter 6), this implied that the solution
to the problem of rioting was to make changes that would reduce the
number of Southern blacks migrating to Northern cities. This solution
would, of course, cause very little inconvenience for Northern mayors
and police chiefs.

In other instances, there are those who have preferred solutions
that they apply to every problem regardless of its nature or empirical
antecedents. For example, the John Birch Society would solve the
problems of racial conflict and the congestion in our cities' judicial
nonsystems by eliminating domestic communism. At the other extreme, certain leaders of the Communist Party in America have suggested that racial conflict and injustice in the courts cannot be reduced
or eliminated until America becomes a classless, socialist society. When
the solution advocated is based upon a value or belief system different
from our own, it is easy for us to spot the preprogrammed nature of
the solution and to call the advocates of such solutions ideologues.
However, it is more difficult to spot the ideological nature of many of
our own pet solutions.

For example, some form of individual or group psychotherapy
either for the people "causing" or those "perceiving" the problem has
been advocated by countless psychologists as a solution to every urban
dilemma discussed in this book. One might even accuse the present
authors of being ideologues because we have proposed "more research"
as an approach to every problem. However, we would point out that

more research is not proposed as a solution in itself but as a means of finding or choosing among solutions. Furthermore, we proposed the implementation of many specific changes along with the necessary research efforts to assess the efficacy of the changes. And we certainly are not suggesting that no changes be made until "all of the facts are known."

In an approach to social problems that is entirely self-serving or one in which the same ideological solution is offered for every problem, the analysis is the servant of the solution. But these are not the only alternatives available. There is a third approach, which attempts to base its analysis upon a careful examination of the most relevant information and to formulate the analysis in such a way that the solution is the product of the analysis, not its determiner.

Psychology and individual psychologists can provide a necessary corrective to the first two approaches (the self-serving and the ideological), and make an important contribution to the third approach. We cannot, of course, contribute an unbiased viewpoint, but can offer one that demands that the human dimension be considered in analyzing the problem and that the available information be scrutinized from several perspectives (see above). Furthermore, we can insist that policymakers consider the psychological impact of various proposed solutions before implementing them.

We should also seek to have various proposed solutions pilot-tested before they are fully implemented. If this is not feasible, we should encourage policymakers to look for existing solutions in which "natural circumstances" are already testing proposed solutions for us. This means that various alternatives, including those that policymakers might exclude on the basis of their common sense or folk wisdom, be tested carefully and evaluated before final decisions are made. As psychologists, we are well suited to contribute to this evaluation process because we are the most experienced of any social scientists in the methods of experimentation with humans. Consequently, we could help political scientists and economists to avoid false starts and errors in the "art" of experimentation (McConahay, 1973). At the same time, we must continue to develop new and better methods of basic research into socially relevant areas if we are to make any major contribution to the development and not just the testing of social policies (Silverman, 1971).

The largest and best-known social pilot experiment of the sort we have in mind was conducted by Mathematica, Incorporated, and the Institute for Research on Poverty of the University of Wisconsin. Known as the New Jersey Negative Income Tax Experiment, this research project was primarily directed at answering one question, "Given a guaranteed annual income, how much, if any, would recipients reduce their work effort?" (Kershaw, 1972). The participants in the study were white, black, and Puerto Rican working-class families living in five cities in New Jersey and Pennsylvania. The families were randomly assigned to one of eight "experimental groups" or to a control group. Those in the experimental groups received one of eight different levels of guaranteed income while control group participants received no extra income. Interviews were conducted with all participants on a periodic basis from 1967 to 1973. Although the data have not yet been completely analyzed, the preliminary results indicate (contrary to the expectations of many economists and political leaders) that a guaranteed income did *not* reduce the amount of money earned through work by the persons in the experimental groups. Nor did the guaranteed income cause a reduction in adherence to the "work ethic." These results strongly suggest that a guaranteed income program would not have a deleterious effect on the work behavior or attitudes of Americans.

BUT WILL THEY BUY IT?

Choosing the best or most appropriate solution to an urban problem is of little value if that solution is never implemented. Most psychologists —and Americans in general—think getting it implemented means selling it to the public. In fact, this is generally thought of as the only point in the process where psychology can make a major contribution. We disagree with both assumptions.

As we have indicated above, psychology should make a contribution to the definition and analysis of problems and to the selection of preferred solutions. To the extent that we are able to make contributions at various early stages in the process, the task of implementing the solutions will be considerably eased.

We also disagree with the assumption that selling the public on a solution is the necessary and sufficient condition for getting it implemented. To get a solution implemented, first the policymakers must be convinced and then those responsible for the day-to-day details of carrying out the policy must be enlisted to help, or at least not hinder, the implementation of the new program. One way to convince policymakers of the soundness of a solution is to show that it is overwhelmingly endorsed by the general public. Yet there are many times when overwhelming public opinion has no effect (the case of gun control is an example) and other times when public opinion changes only after the policies have been implemented by government or other powerful segments of our society [for example, desegregation in the South (see Sheatsley, 1966)].

Psychologists have studied attitude and behavior change and can make contributions to influencing public opinion (Lane & Sears, 1964); we also know something about mobilizing aggrieved persons into becoming pressure groups and political blocs that can force (or at least make it easier for) the government to implement certain policies. All too often, however, we have used our skills only to "help" aggrieved groups to adjust. What we could do, to use Archibald's (1970) analogy, is to organize people to force society to give them new shoes rather than alter their feet to fit the shoes that are available. For example, psychologist Hannah Levin (1970) has described one successful effort by what she calls "radical professionals" to organize and help the poor to gain more control over their immediate community mental health services. As a result of their success, the poor people involved became politicized and began pressuring the city and national governments for a reordering of priorities and a redistribution of power in other spheres.

Finally, once leaders have been convinced (or forced) to accept innovation, psychologists can contribute to the task of selling the new policies and procedures to the persons who must implement them (teachers, welfare workers, policemen, etc.). A study by Coch and French (1948) provides a good example of how this might be done. These researchers found it advantageous to include the persons concerned with implementing changes in the planning and conducting of the changes. Such participation accords well with the humanistic and democratic values held by most psychologists and it also happens to be an efficient and productive way to introduce change. Industrial psychologists have been working on such problems for years and could make an important contribution in this area.

THE CONTEXT FOR FINDING SOLUTIONS

In addition to working directly toward finding solutions to our current urban problems (and those that new social and technological forces will create in the future) and for the adoption of the best solutions by lobbying, selling, and mobilizing the aggrieved to struggle for redress, there is another contribution psychologists can make to the solution of our urban dilemmas. We can help to create or foster an atmosphere in which political conflict can be conducted in a "civil" way. With the collaboration of political scientists, psychologists can help create new curricula for elementary and high school social studies or American government classes that will make use of what we already know about dealing with political and social conflict.

Today's schools, for the most part fail to educate students to be the kind of citizens who can live in and foster a climate in which real conflict can be resolved in an open, nonviolent fashion. Their failure is summed up in three important points made by Robert D. Hess (1968) about the current state of the political education of our children. First, schools encourage a passive acceptance of the status quo. They do a good job of inculcating a generalized positive feeling for one's country and its symbols, for example, the flag, and a faith in political authority, particularly the presidency (Sears, 1969). However, schools do not prepare our children to cope with a world filled with problems. Teachers do not think children, especially those in grades one through three, should be exposed to touchy issues, e.g., race relations, politics, poverty. The result is that the children (particularly those whose home environment corresponds to the positively pictured status quo) see the present state of affairs as perfectly acceptable.

Second, schools present voting as almost the only way (and certainly the *best* way) to participate in the process of government. They generally neglect questions of how to influence officials once they are elected, and there is almost no mention of political influence through coalitions and pressure groups. Lobbying by interest groups, for example, is an almost forbidden topic.

A third aspect of the school in relation to political socialization is that the school plays down conflict within the system. Children are taught that candidates and parties debate issues before elections, but that after elections everyone joins hands and America marches forward. This ignores the existing conflict for scarce resources (e.g., economic and political power) and researchers have suggested that it produces adults who are afraid to face conflict themselves and who reject those who point to its existence (Hess, 1968; Zellman & Sears, 1971).

The weaknesses in political education have grave consequences for urban problems in general. Those who accept the status quo (especially if they live in the suburbs) will find it hard to understand all the talk about "city problems" and the need to plan future development on a metropolitan basis (i.e., city plus suburbs). Those who want to change the city may concentrate on the vote rather than on identifying the important and influencible parts of existing school, housing, and other bureaucracies. Perhaps most importantly, those who have not learned that real conflict is a fundamental part both of the political process and of problem solution, will either run from, ignore, or seek to suppress controversies over issues such as busing or scatter-site housing. Hence, the fact of controversy instead of the proposed solutions may become the issue, and important suggestions and proposals may be suppressed or go unheard.

The civics or government curriculum of our schools should be altered in at least two major ways. First, conflict within our political system should be discussed honestly and forthrightly. Zellman and Sears (1971) report that such a curriculum has been successfully developed for fifth- through ninth-graders and that the program appears to have the side benefit of increasing the students' tolerance for civil liberties. Second, school children should be taught how all levels of government work. This means not only a discussion of the three branches of the federal government and other aspects of the formal system, but also coverage of the informal system, e.g., lobbying, trading votes, regional, and other special interest coalitions.

If implemented, these two curricular changes could help produce the kind of citizenry necessary to foster a climate in which we could find long-term solutions not only to our urban dilemmas but also to the broader problems of intergroup hostility, environmental pollution, and the population explosion.

A FINAL WORD

As we indicated in Chapter 1, writing this textbook has not been easy, for we have fluctuated throughout between moods of slight optimism and those of deep pessimism. If we have been too pessimistic in earlier chapters we have probably been too optimistic in this one. The political system is far more complex than we have described it in this chapter, and selling any given reform, no matter how psychologically sound and empirically validated it may appear to us, could prove to be a herculean task. Yet we do not know how hard or complicated the task will be until we begin it.

In addition to optimism and pessimism, we have also fluctuated between the poles of individual change and system change. Our discussion of political education is a good example. Though we have tended to downgrade attempts to deal with the urban dilemmas by changing individuals because we felt that psychology was already too biased in that direction, we have suggested that our country could introduce a climate for finding long-term solutions by teaching citizens to be more tolerant and to deal with conflict in a civil fashion. That is, we suggested a system change (a new way of teaching civics) intended ultimately to change individuals (the students who will become citizens). We want to suggest that while the dichotomy of individual change and system change is a useful one for discussing social change, we need not be limited to either one line of attack or the other. We need to change both individuals *and* systems and we need multiple approaches to changing both.

We have proposed many specific reforms or changes and many more general ones. All of these (and more) are required if we are to solve our urban dilemmas. No single change will be successful in the absence of other changes.

In short, what we are calling for is an approach incorporating the features of Campbell's experimenting society (1969, also see Chapter 1) in which the commitment is not to one particular solution or set of solutions but to finding the best solution.

References

Aberbach, J. D., and J. L. Walker: "The Meanings of Black Power: A Comparison of White and Black Interpretations of a Political Slogan," *The American Political Science Review*, **64**:367–388, 1970*a*.

Aberbach, J. D., and J. C. Walker: "Political Trust and Racial Ideology," *American Political Science Review*, **64**:1199–1219, 1970*b*.

Allen, V. L.: "Personality Correlates of Poverty," in V. L. Allen (ed.), *Psychological Factors in Poverty*, Markham Publishing Co., Chicago, 1970, pp. 242–266.

Allport, G.: *The Nature of Prejudice*, Doubleday, New York, 1958.

Alsop, J.: "Ghetto Education. Joseph Alsop Replies to His Critics," *The New Republic*, 18–23, November 18, 1967.

Anderson, P.: "The Pot Lobby," *New York Times Magazine*, January 21, 1973, p. 8 passim.

Aptheker, H.: *History of Negro Slave Revolts*, International Publishers, New York, 1969.

Archibald, K.: "Alternative Orientations to Social Science Utilization," *Social Science Information*, **9**:7–34, 1970.

Ares, C. E., A. Rankin, and H. Sturz: "The Manhattan Bail Project: An

Interim Report on the Use of Pretrial Parole," *New York University Law Review,* 38:67–92, 1963.

Ashmore, R. D.: "Prejudice: Causes and Cures," in B. E. Collins, *Social Psychology,* Addison-Wesley, Reading, Mass., 1970, pp. 243–339.

Ashmore, R. D., and R. J. Butsch: "Perceived Threat and the Perception of Violence in Biracial Settings: Toward an Experimental Paradigm," paper presented at the Eastern Psychological Association Convention, April, 1972, Boston.

Ashmore, R. D., F. Turner, D. A. Donato, and T. Nevenglosky: "How White Americans View the Concept of Black Power," unpublished manuscript, Rutgers University, 1973.

Backman, C. W., and P. F. Secord: *A Social Psychological View of Education,* Harcourt, Brace and World, New York, 1968.

Baratz, J. C.: "Teaching Reading in an Urban Negro School System," in F. Williams (ed.), *Language and Poverty,* Markham Publishing Co., Chicago, 1970.

Baratz, S. S., and J. C. Baratz: "Early Childhood Intervention: The Social Science Base of Institutional Racism," *Harvard Educational Review,* 40:29–47, 1970.

Baratz, S. S., and R. Shuy (eds.): *Teaching Black Children to Read,* Center for Applied Linguistics, Washington, D.C., 1969.

Beardwood, R.: "The New Negro Mood," *Fortune,* 78:146 passim, 1968.

Becker, H. S.: "The Career of the Chicago Public School Teacher," *American Sociological Review,* 17:470–476, 1952.

Becker, H. S.: *Outsiders,* The Free Press, New York, 1963.

Beez, W. V.: "Influence of Biased Psychological Reports on Teachers' Behavior and Pupil Performance," in M. B. Miles and W. W. Charters (eds.), *Learning in Social Settings,* Allyn and Bacon, Inc., Boston, 1970.

Bettelheim, B.: "Individual and Mass Behavior in Extreme Situations," *Journal of Abnormal and Social Psychology,* 48:417–452, 1943.

Birch, H. G., and J. D. Gussow: *Disadvantaged Children,* Harcourt, Brace and World, New York, 1970.

Black, D. J., and A. J. Reiss, Jr.: "Patterns of Behavior in Police and Citizen Transactions," a report of a research study submitted to The President's Commission on Law Enforcement and Administration of Justice, Washington, D.C., 1967.

Blum, Z. D., and P. H. Rossi: "Social Class Research and Images of the Poor: A Bibliographic Review," in D. P. Moynihan (ed.),

On Understanding Poverty: Perspectives from the Social Sciences, Basic Books, New York, 1968, pp. 343-397.

Blumenthal, R.: "Porno Chic," *New York Times Magazine,* January 21, 1973, p. 28 passim.

Brown, R.: *Social Psychology,* The Free Press, New York, 1965.

Burnham, W. D.: *Critical Elections and the Main Springs of American Politics,* W. W. Norton, New York, 1970.

Calhoun, J. B.: "Population Density and Social Pathology," *Scientific American,* 206:139-148, 1962.

Campbell, A.: *White Attitudes Toward Black People,* Institute for Social Research, University of Michigan, Ann Arbor, 1971.

Campbell, A., and H. Schuman: "Racial Attitudes in Fifteen American Cities," *Supplemental Studies for the National Advisory Commission on Civil Disorders,* Washington, D.C., 1968, pp. 1-67.

Campbell, D. T.: "The Experimenting Society," paper presented at the 1969 American Psychological Association Convention, Washington, D.C.

Campbell, J., J. Sahid, and S. Stang (eds.): *Law and Order Reconsidered,* U.S. Government Printing Office, Washington, D.C., 1969.

Cantril, A. H.: *The Pattern of Human Concerns,* Rutgers University Press, New Brunswick, N.J., 1965.

Cantril, A. H., and C. W. Roll, Jr.: *Hopes and Fears of the American People,* Universe Books, New York, 1971.

Caplan, N.: "The New Ghetto Man: A Review of Recent Empirical Studies," *Journal of Social Issues,* 26:59-73, 1970.

Caplan, N., and S. D. Nelson: "On Being Useful: The Nature and Consequences of Psychological Research on Social Problems," *The American Psychologist,* 28:199-211, 1973.

Caplan, N., and J. M. Paige: "A Study of Ghetto Rioters," *Scientific American,* 219:15-21, 1968.

Caplovitz, D.: "Economic Aspects of Poverty," in V. L. Allen (ed.), *Psychological Factors in Poverty,* Markham Publishing Company, Chicago, 1970.

Caprio, R. J.: "Place Utility, Social Obsolescence, and Qualitative Housing Change," *Proceedings of the Association of American Geographers,* 4:14-19, 1972.

Carey, G. W.: "Density, Crowding, Stress, and the Ghetto," *American Behavioral Scientist,* 15:495-509, 1972.

Carmichael, S., and C. V. Hamilton: *Black Power: The Politics of Liberation in America,* Vintage Books, New York, 1967.

Casper, J. D.: *American Criminal Justice: The Defendant's Perspective,* Prentice-Hall, Englewood Cliffs, N.J., 1972.

Census of Governments, vol. 6, no. 5, 1967.

Center for Research in Marketing, *Congressional Quarterly,* weekly report no. 36, September 8, 1967.

Chesler, M. A., S. Wittes, and N. Radin: "When Northern Schools Desegregate," *American Education,* 4:12–15, 1968.

Christian, J. J.: "The Pathology of Overpopulation," *Military Medicine,* 128:571–603, 1963.

Cicourel, A., and J. L. Kituse: *Educational Decision-makers,* Bobbs-Merrill, New York, 1963.

Clark, K. B.: *Dark Ghetto: Dilemmas of Social Power,* Harper and Row, New York, 1967.

Clark, K. B., and M. P. Clark: "Racial Identification and Preference in Negro Children," in T. M. Newcomb and E. L. Hartley (eds.), *Readings in Social Psychology,* Holt, Rinehart and Winston, New York, 1947.

Clausen, J. A.: "Drug Use," in R. K. Merton and R. Nisbet (eds.), *Contemporary Social Problems,* 3rd ed., Harcourt Brace Jovanovich, New York, 1971, pp. 185–226.

Cloward, R. A., and J. A. Jones: "Social Class: Educational Attitudes and Participation," in A. H. Passow (ed.), *Education in Depressed Areas,* Teachers College Press, Columbia University, New York, 1963.

Coch, L., and J. R. P. French: "Overcoming Resistance to Change," *Human Relations,* 1:512–532, 1948.

Cohen, A. K., and J. F. Short, Jr.: *Crime and Juvenile Delinquency,* in R. K. Merton and R. Nisbet (eds.), *Contemporary Social Problems,* 3rd ed., Harcourt Brace Jovanovich, New York, 1971, pp. 89–146.

Coleman, J. S.: *Resources for Social Change: Race in the United States,* Wiley-Interscience, New York, 1971.

Coleman, J. S., et al.: *Equality of Educational Opportunity,* United States Government Printing Office, Washington, D.C., 1966.

Coles, R.: *The South Goes North (Volume III of Children of Crisis),* Little, Brown and Company, Boston, 1967.

Colle, R. D.: "Color on T.V.," *The Reporter,* November 30, 1967, pp. 23–25.

Collins, B. E.: *Social Psychology,* Addison-Wesley, Reading, Mass., 1970.

Cressey, D. R., and D. A. Ward: *Delinquency, Crime, and Social Process,* Harper, New York, 1969.

Davis, F. J.: "Crime News in Colorado Newspapers," *American Journal of Sociology*, **57**:325–330, 1952.

Davis, K. E.: "Drug Effects and Drug Use," in L. S. Wrightsman, *Social Psychology in the Seventies*, Brooks/Cole, Monterey, Calif. 1972, pp. 517–548.

deCharms, R.: "Personal Causation Training in Schools," *Journal of Applied Social Psychology*, **2**:95–113, 1972.

Deevey, E. S., Jr.: "The Human Population," *Scientific American*, **203**:194–204, 1960.

Deutsch, M.: "Social Intervention and the Malleability of the Child," in M. Deutsch, *The Disadvantaged Child*, Basic Books, New York, 1967, pp. 3–29.

Dobrovir, W.: "The Problem of Overcriminalization," in J. Campbell, J. Sahid, and S. Stang (eds.), *Law and Order Reconsidered*, U.S. Government Printing Office, Washington, D.C., 1969, pp. 551–570.

Dollard, J.: *Caste and Class in a Southern Town*, Yale University Press, New Haven, 1937.

Donnerstein, E., M. Donnerstein, M. Simon, and R. Ditrichs: "Variables in Interracial Aggression: Expected Retaliation and a Riot," *Journal of Personality and Social Psychology*, **22**:236–245, 1972.

Duncan, O. D.: "Inheritance of Poverty or Inheritance of Race?," in D. P. Moynihan (ed.), *On Understanding Poverty: Perspectives from the Social Sciences*, Basic Books, New York, 1968, pp. 85–110.

Dyer, H. S.: "School Factors and Educational Opportunity," *Harvard Educational Review*, **38**:38–56, 1968.

Edelman, M.: *Politics as Symbolic Action*, Markham Publishing Company, Chicago, 1971.

Ellison, R.: *The Invisible Man*, Random House, New York, 1952 (original copyright 1947).

FBI: *Uniform Crime Reports*, 1970.

Feagin, J. R.: "Poverty: We Still Believe That God Helps Those Who Help Themselves," *Psychology Today*, **6**:101–110, 129, 1972.

Fiedler, F. E., T. R. Mitchell, and H. Triandis: "The Culture Assimilator: An Approach to Cross-cultural Training," *Journal of Applied Psychology*, **55**:95–102, 1971.

Fleming, E. S., and R. G. Anttonen: "Teacher Expectancy or My Fair Lady," *American Educational Research Journal*, **8**:241–252, 1971.

Fogelson, R. M., and R. B. Hill: "Who Riots? A Study of Participation in 1967 Riots," in *Supplemental Studies for the National Advisory Commission on Civil Disorders*, 1968, pp. 217–248.

Foote, C.: "A Study of the Administration of Bail in New York City," *University of Pennsylvania Law Review*, **106**:685–730, 1958.

Franklin, R. D.: "Youth's Expectancies About Internal Versus External Control of Reinforcement Related to N Variables," doctoral dissertation, Purdue University, 1963.

Freed, D. J.: "The Nonsystem of Criminal Justice," in J. Campbell, J. Sahid, and S. Stang (eds.), *Law and Order Reconsidered*, U.S. Government Printing Office, Washington, D.C., 1969, pp. 265–284.

Freed, D. J., and P. Wald: *Bail in the United States: 1964*, Record Press, New York, 1964.

Freedman, J. L.: "A Positive View of Population Density," *Psychology Today*, September, 1971, pp. 58 passim.

Freedman, J. L., S. Klevansky, and P. R. Ehrlich: "The Effect of Crowding on Human Task Performance," *Journal of Applied Social Psychology*, **1**:7–25, 1971.

Freedman, J. L., A. S. Levy, R. W. Buchanan, and J. Price: "Crowding and Human Aggressiveness," *Journal of Experimental Social Psychology*, **8**:528–548, 1972.

Friedman, L. S.: "Economics and Reform in the System of Criminal Justice," in *A Working Paper of the Center for the Study of the City and Its Environment*, Institution for Social and Policy Studies, Yale University, New Haven, 1972.

Galle, O. R., W. R. Gove, and J. M. McPherson: "Population Density and Pathology: What Are the Relations for Man?," *Science*, **176**:23–30, 1972.

Gallup, G.: *Gallup Opinion Index*, March, 1969, no. 45, p. 12.

Gallup, G.: *Gallup Opinion Index*, August, 1972, no. 86, p. 23.

Gans, H. J.: "Culture and Class in the Study of Poverty: An Approach to Anti-poverty Research," in D. P. Moynihan (ed.), *On Understanding Poverty: Perspectives from the Social Sciences*, Basic Books, Inc., New York, 1968.

Gans, H. J.: "The Positive Functions of Poverty," *American Journal of Sociology*, **78**:275–289, 1972.

Gentry, A., B. Jones, C. Peele, R. Phillips, J. Woodbury, and R. Woodbury: *Urban Education: The Hope Factor*, W. B. Saunders, Philadelphia, 1972.

Getzels, J. W., and P. W. Jackson: "The Teacher's Personality and Characteristics," in N. L. Gage (ed.), *Handbook of Research on Teaching*, Rand McNally, Chicago, 1963, pp. 506–582.

Gilbert, G. M.: "Stereotype Persistence and Change Among College Students," *Journal of Abnormal and Social Psychology*, **46**:245–254, 1951.

Gladwin, T.: *Poverty USA*, Little, Brown and Co., Boston, 1967.

Glass, D. C., and J. E. Singer: *Urban Stress*, Academic Press, New York, 1972.

Goldberg, M. L.: "Socio-psychological Issues in the Education of the Disadvantaged," in A. H. Passow (ed.), *Urban Education in the 1970's*, Teachers College Press, Columbia University, New York, 1971, pp. 61–93.

Goldenberg, I. I.: *Reading in the First Grade: An Observational Study of the Hypothesis of the Self-Fulfilling Prophecy*, unpublished manuscript, Yale University.

Goldsby, R. A.: *Race and Racism*, Macmillan, New York, 1971.

Goode, W. J.: "Family Disorganization," in R. K. Merton and R. Nisbet (eds.), *Contemporary Social Problems*, 3rd ed., Harcourt Brace Jovanovich, New York, 1971, pp. 467–544.

Goodman, M. E.: *Race Awareness in Young Children*, Collier Books, New York, 1964.

Goodwin, L.: *Do the Poor Want to Work?*, The Brookings Institution, Washington, D.C., 1972.

Gordon, M. M.: *Assimilation in American Life: The Role of Race, Religion, and National Origins*, Oxford University Press, New York, 1964.

Gore, P. M., and J. B. Rotter: "A Personality Correlate of Social Action," *Journal of Personality*, 31:58–64, 1963.

Governor's Commission on Los Angeles Riots (McCone Commission): *Violence in the City–an End or a Beginning?*, Los Angeles, 1966.

Greeley, A. M., and P. B. Sheatsley: "Attitudes Toward Racial Integration," *Scientific American*, 225:13–19, 1971.

Griffitt, W., and R. Veitch: "Hot and Crowded: Influences of Population Density and Temperature on Interpersonal Affective Behavior," *Journal of Personality and Social Psychology*, 17:92–98, 1971.

Groves, W. E., and P. H. Rossi: "Police Perceptions of a Hostile Ghetto: Realism or Projection?," *American Behavioral Scientist*, 13:727–743, 1970.

Gurin, G.: *Inner-city Negro Youth in a Job Training Project: A Study of Factors Related to Attrition and Job Success*, Institute for Social Research, Ann Arbor, Michigan, 1968.

Hammond, A. L.: "Computer-assisted Instructions: Many Efforts, Mixed Results," *Science*, 176:1005–1006, 1972.

Harrington, M.: *The Other America*, Macmillan, New York, 1962.

Harris, L.: "Racial Stereotypes at Heart of Communication Gap,"

The Home News, New Brunswick, N.J., vol. 93(209): October 5, 1971.

Hartung, F. E.: "The White Collar Thief," in D. R. Cressey and D. A. Ward (eds.), *Delinquency, Crime, and Social Process,* Harper and Row, New York, 1969, pp. 1103–1113.

Heider, F.: "Social Perception and Phenomenal Causality," *Psychological Review,* 51:358–374, 1944.

Hess, R. D.: "Political Socialization in the Schools," *Harvard Educational Review,* 38:528–535, 1968.

Hsu, F. L. K.: "American Core Value and National Character," in F. L. K. Hsu (ed.), *Psychological Anthropology,* Schenkman Publishing Co., Cambridge, Mass., 1972, pp. 241–262.

Jacobs, P.: *Prelude to Riot,* Vintage, New York, 1967.

Jensen, A. R.: "How Much Can We Boost I.Q. and Scholastic Achievement?," *Harvard Educational Review,* 39:1–23, 1969.

John, V. P., and V. M. Horner: "Bilingualism and the Spanish Speaking Child," in F. Williams (ed.), *Language and Poverty,* Markham Publishing Company, Chicago, 1970.

Johnson, D. A., R. J. Porter, and P. L. Mateljan: "Racial Discrimination in Apartment Rentals," *Journal of Applied Social Psychology,* 1:364–377, 1971.

Johnson, P. B., D. O. Sears, and J. B. McConahay: "Black Invisibility, the Press, and the Los Angeles Riot," *The American Journal of Sociology,* 76:698–721, 1971.

Johnson, T. J., R. Feigenbaum, and M. Weiby: "Some Determinants and Consequences of the Teacher's Perception of Causation," *Journal of Educational Psychology,* 55:237–246, 1964.

Johnson, W. A.: *A Comparison of the Philosophies of Human Nature of Negro and White High School Seniors,* unpublished Master's thesis, George Peabody College for Teachers, 1969.

Jones, E. E., and K. E. Davis: "From Acts to Dispositions: The Attribution Process in Person Perception," in L. Berkowitz (ed.), *Advances in Experimental Social Psychology,* vol. II, Academic Press, New York, 1965, pp. 219–266.

Jones, E. E., E. E. Kanouse, H. H. Kelley, R. E. Nisbett, S. Valins, and B. Weiner: *Attribution: Perceiving the Causes of Behavior,* General Learning Press, Morristown, N.J., 1972.

Jones, J.: *Prejudice and Racism,* Addison-Wesley, Reading, Mass., 1972.

Kane, M. B.: *Minorities in Textbooks,* Quadrangle Books, Chicago, 1970.

Karlins, M., T. Coffman, and G. Walters: "On the Fading of Social Stereotypes: Studies in Three Generations of College Students," *Journal of Personality and Social Psychology*, 13:1–16, 1969.

Katz, D., and J. Braly: "Verbal Stereotypes and Racial Prejudice," *Journal of Abnormal and Social Psychology*, 30:175–193, 1933.

Katz, E., and J. J. Feldman: "The Debates in the Light of Research: A Survey of Surveys," in S. Kraus (ed.), *The Great Debates*, Indiana University Press, Bloomington, 1962, pp. 173–223.

Kelley, H. H.: "Attribution Theory in Social Psychology," in D. Levine (ed.), *Nebraska Symposium on Motivation 1967*, University of Nebraska Press, Lincoln, Neb., 1967, pp. 192–240.

Kershaw, D. N.: "A Negative Income Tax Experiment," *Scientific American*, 227:19–25, 1972.

King, M. L., Jr.: *Where Do We Go From Here: Chaos or Community?*, Beacon Press, Boston, 1967.

Kinsey, A. C., W. B. Pomroy, and C. E. Martin: *Sexual Behavior in the Human Male*, W. B. Saunders Co., Philadelphia, 1948.

Kleiner, R. J., and S. Parker: "Social-psychological Aspects of Migration and Mental Disorder in a Negro Population," *American Behavioral Scientist*, 13:104–125, 1969.

Knowles, L. L., and K. Prewitt (eds.): *Institutional Racism in America*, Prentice-Hall, Englewood Cliffs, N.J., 1969.

Kohl, H.: *36 Children*, The New American Library, New York, 1968.

Kornberg, L.: "Meaningful Teachers for Alienated Children," in A. H. Passow (ed.), *Education in Depressed Areas*, Teachers College Press, Columbia University, N.Y., 1963, pp. 262–278.

Lane, R. E.: *Political Ideology*, Free Press of Glencoe, New York, 1962.

Lane, R. E., and D. O. Sears: *Public Opinion*, Prentice-Hall, Englewood Cliffs, N.J., 1964.

LEAA: Expenditure and Employment Data for the Criminal Justice System, 1968-69 and 1969-70, U.S. Government Printing Office, Washington, D.C., 1971.

Legant, P.: "The Deserving Victim: The Effects of Length of Pretrial Detention, Crime Severity, and Juror Attitudes on Simulated Jury Decisions," unpublished doctoral dissertation, Yale University, New Haven, 1973.

Levin, H. (ed.): *Community Control of Schools*, Brookings Institution, Washington, D.C., 1970.

Lewis, O.: "The Culture of Poverty," in D. P. Moynihan (ed.), *On*

Understanding Poverty: Perspectives from the Social Sciences, Basic Books, New York, 1968, pp. 187-200.

Lewis, O.: *Five Families: Mexican Case Studies in the Culture of Poverty,* Basic Books, New York, 1959.

Lewis, O.: *La Vida: A Puerto Rican Family in the Culture of Poverty,* Random House, New York, 1966.

Lichter, J. H., and D. W. Johnson: "Changes in Attitudes toward Negroes of White Elementary School Students after Use of Multi-ethnic Readers," *Journal of Educational Psychology,* 60:148-152, 1969.

Liebow, E.: *Tally's Corner: A Study of Negro Streetcorner Men,* Little, Brown, Boston, 1967.

McConahay, J. B.: "Experimental Research," in J. N. Knutson (ed.), *Handbook of Political Psychology,* Jossey-Bass, San Francisco, 1973, pp. 356-382.

Matza, D.: "Poverty and Disrepute," in R. K. Merton and R. Nisbet (eds.), *Contemporary Social Problems,* 3rd ed., Harcourt Brace Jovanovich, New York, 1971, pp. 601-656.

Mendelsohn, R. A.: "Police-Community Relations: A Need in Search of Police Support," *American Behavioral Scientist,* 13:745-760, 1970.

Milbrath, L. W.: *Political Participation,* Rand McNally, Chicago, 1965.

Milgram, S.: "The Experience of Living in Cities," *Science,* 167: 1461-1468, 1970.

Milgram, S.: "Some Conditions of Obedience and Disobedience to Authority," in I. D. Steiner and M. Fishbein (eds.), *Current Studies in Social Psychology,* Holt, Rinehart and Winston, New York, 1965, pp. 243-262.

Miller, S. M., and F. Riessman: *Social Class and Social Policy,* Basic Books, New York, 1968.

Mitchell, R. E.: "Some Social Implications of High Density Housing," *American Sociological Review,* 36:18-29, 1971.

Morris, R., and V. Jefferies: "The White Reaction Study," in N. E. Cohen (ed.), *The Los Angeles Riots: A Socio-psychological Study,* Praeger, New York, 1970, pp. 480-601.

Murphy, R. J., and J. W. Watson: "The Structure of Discontent: The Relationship Between Social Structure, Grievance, and Riot Support," in N. E. Cohen (ed.), *The Los Angeles Riots: A Socio-psychological Study,* Praeger, New York, 1970, pp. 140-257.

Nagel, S. S.: "The Tipped Scales of American Justice," *Transaction,* May/June, 1966.

National Advisory Commission on Civil Disorders (NACCD): *Report of the National Advisory Commission on Civil Disorders* (Kerner Commission Report), 1968.

National Advisory Commission on Rural Poverty: *The People Left Behind,* Washington, D.C., 1967.

Nisbett, R. F., C. Caputo, P. Legant, and J. Marecek: "Behavior As Seen by the Actor and As Seen by the Observer," *Journal of Personality and Social Psychology,* 27:154–164, 1973.

Ogletree, E.: "Ability Grouping: Its Effects on Attitudes," *Journal of Social Psychology,* 82:137–138, 1970.

Packer, H.: *The Limits of Criminal Sanctions,* Stanford University Press, Stanford, 1968.

Paige, J. M.: "Changing Patterns of Anti-white Attitudes Among Blacks," *Journal of Social Issues,* 26:69–86, 1970.

Parker, S., and R. J. Kleiner: *Mental Illness in the Urban Negro Community,* Free Press, New York, 1966.

Perlman, D., and S. Oskamp: "The Effects of Picture Content and Exposure Frequency on Evaluations of Negroes and Whites," *Journal of Experimental Social Psychology,* 7:503–514, 1971.

Pettigrew, T. F.: *A Profile of the Negro American,* Van Nostrand, Princeton, N.J., 1964.

Pettigrew, T. F.: *Racially Separate or Together?,* McGraw Hill, New York, 1971.

Pettigrew, T. F.: "Social Evaluation Theory: Convergences and Applications," in D. Levine (ed.), *Nebraska Symposium on Motivation 1967,* University of Nebraska Press, Lincoln, Neb. 1967.

Pinkney, A.: *Black Americans,* Prentice-Hall, Englewood Cliffs, N.J., 1969.

Platt, A. M.: *The Politics of Riot Commissions,* Collier Books, New York, 1971.

Rabinowitz, F. F., and J. La Mare: "After Suburbia, What?: The New Communities Movement in Los Angeles," in W. Z. Hirsch (ed.), *Los Angeles: Viability and Prospects of Metropolitan Leadership,* Praeger, New York, 1971, pp. 133–168.

Rainwater, L.: *Behind Ghetto Walls,* Aldine Publishing Company, Chicago, 1970.

Rainwater, L.: "The Problem of Lower-class Culture and Poverty-War Strategy," in D. P. Moynihan, (ed.), *On Understanding Poverty: Perspectives from the Social Sciences,* Basic Books, New York, 1968, pp. 229–259.

Rainwater, L.: "Some Aspects of Lower Class Sexual Behavior," *Journal of Social Issues,* 22:96–108, 1966.

Rankin, A.: "The Effect of Pretrial Detention," *New York University Law Review,* 641–655, June 1964.

Rist, R. C.: "Student Social Class and Teacher Expectations: The Self-fulfilling Prophesy in Ghetto Education," *Harvard Educational Review,* 40:411–451, 1970.

Robinson, J. P., and P. R. Shaver: *Measures of Social Psychological Attitudes,* Institute for Social Research, University of Michigan, Ann Arbor, 1969.

Rokeach, M., and S. Parker: *Values as Social Indicators of Poverty and Race Relations in America,* unpublished manuscript, 1970.

Rosenfeld, G.: *Shut Those Thick Lips! A Study of Slum School Failure,* Holt, Rinehart and Winston, New York, 1971.

Rosenthal, R. R.: *Experimenter Effects in Behavioral Research,* Appleton-Century-Crofts, New York, 1966.

Rosenthal, R. R., and L. Jacobson: *Pygmalion in the Classroom,* Holt, Rinehart and Winston, New York, 1968.

Ross, R., and G. L. Staines: "The Politics of Analyzing Social Problems," *Social Problems,* 20:18–40, 1972.

Rossi, P. H., and Z. D. Blum: "Class, Status and Poverty," in D. P. Moynihan (ed.), *On Understanding Poverty: Perspectives from the Social Sciences,* Basic Books, New York, 1968, pp. 36–63.

Roth, T., M. Kramer, and J. Tinder: "Noise–Sleep, and Post Sleep Behavior," paper delivered to the American Psychiatric Association, Washington, D.C., 1971.

Rubovits, P. C., and M. L. Maehr: "Pygmalion Analyzed: Toward an Explanation of the Rosenthal-Jacobson Findings," *Journal of Personality and Social Psychology,* 19:197–203, 1971.

Ryan, W.: *Blaming the Victim,* Pantheon, New York, 1971.

Schachter, S.: *The Psychology of Affiliation,* Stanford University Press, Palo Alto, California, 1959.

Schiltz, M. E.: *Public Attitudes Toward Social Security, 1935–1956,* U.S. Government Printing Office, Washington, D.C., 1970.

Schmitt, R. C.: "Density, Delinquency and Crime in Honolulu," *Sociology and Social Research,* 41:274–276, 1957.

Schmitt, R. C.: "Density, Health and Social Disorganization," *Journal of American Institute of Planners,* 32:38–40, 1966.

Schubert, G.: "Judicial Process and Behavior, 1963–1971," in J. A. Robinson (ed.), *Political Science Annual,* vol. 3, Bobbs-Merrill, Indianapolis, 1972, pp. 210–280.

Schuchter, A.: *White Power/Black Freedom,* Beacon Press, Boston, 1968.

Schuman, H.: "Free Will and Determinism in Public Beliefs About Race," unpublished paper, University of Michigan, 1969.

Schwartz, M. A.: *Trends in White Attitudes Toward Negroes,* National Opinion Research, Chicago, 1967.

Schwartz, R. D., and J. H. Skolnick: "A Study of Legal Stigma," *Social Problems,* 10:133–138, 1962.

Sears, D. O.: "Political Behavior," in G. Lindzey and E. Aronson (eds.), *The Handbook of Social Psychology,* 2nd ed., vol. 5, Addison-Wesley, Reading, Mass., 1969, pp. 315–458.

Sears, D. O., and D. R. Kinder: "Racial Tensions and Voting in Los Angeles," in W. Z. Hirsch (ed.), *Los Angeles: Viability and Prospects for Metropolitan Leadership,* Praeger, New York, 1971, pp. 51–88.

Sears, D. O., and J. B. McConahay: *The Politics of Violence: The New Urban Blacks and the Watts Riot,* Houghton Mifflin, Boston, 1973.

Sears, D. O., and T. M. Tomlinson: "Riot Ideology in Los Angeles: A Study of Negro Attitudes," *Social Science Quarterly,* 49:485–503, 1968.

Seiver, D. A.: *Density and Fetal Mortality in the United States: 1960,* Yale University Institution for Social and Policy Studies, March 1971.

Sexton, P. C.: *Education and Income: Inequalities of Opportunity in Our Public Schools,* Viking Press, New York, 1961.

Sheatsley, P. B.: "White Attitudes toward the Negro," *Daedelus,* 95:217–238, 1966.

Shively, W. P.: "'Ecological' Inference: The Use of Aggregate Data to Study Individuals," *American Political Science Review,* 63:1183–1196, 1969.

Silberman, C. E.: *Crisis in the Classroom: The Remaking of American Education,* Random House, New York, 1970.

Silverman, I.: "Crisis in Social Psychology: The Relevance of Relevance," *American Psychologist,* 26:583–584, 1971.

Singer, L. R.: "The Bail Problem: Release or Detention Before Trial," in J. Campbell, J. Sahid, and S. Stang (eds.), *Law and Order Reconsidered,* U.S. Government Printing Office, Washington, D.C., 1969, pp. 427–467.

Snow, R. E.: "Unfinished Pygmalion," *Contemporary Psychology,* 14:197–200, 1969.

Starr, R., and J. Carlson: "Pollution and Poverty: The Strategy of Cross Commitment," *The Public Interest*, 104–131, Winter 1968.

Statistical Abstracts of the United States, 1971.

Sternlieb, G. S., and B. P. Indik: *The Ecology of Welfare: Housing and the Welfare Crisis in New York City*, Transaction Books, New Brunswick, N.J., 1973.

Stevenson, H. W., and E. C. Stewart: "A Developmental Study of Racial Awareness in Young Children," *Child Development*, 29:399–410, 1958.

Stokols, D.: "On the Distinction Between Density and Crowding: Some Implications for Future Research," *Psychological Review*, 79: 275–277, 1972.

Suppes, P., and M. Morningstar: "Technological Innovations: Computer-assisted Instruction and Compensatory Education," in F. K. Korten, S. W. Cook, and J. Lacey (eds.), *Psychology and the Problems of Society*, American Psychological Association, Washington, D.C., 1970.

Taeuber, K. E.: "Population Trends of the 1960's," *Science*, 176: 773–777, 1972.

Taeuber, K. E.: "Residential Segregation," *Scientific American*, 213: 1965.

Taeuber, K. E., and A. F. Taeuber: "The Negro Population in the United States," in J. P. Davis (ed.), *The American Negro Reference Book*, Prentice-Hall, Englewood Cliffs, N.J., 1966.

Tager, J., and P. D. Goist (eds.): *The Urban Vision: Selected Interpretations of the Modern American City*, Dorsey Press, Homewood, Ill., 1970.

Thibaut, J. W., and H. H. Kelley: *The Social Psychology of Groups*, Wiley, New York, 1959.

Tucker, J., and T. S. Friedman: "Population Density and Group Size," *American Journal of Sociology*, 77:742–746, 1972.

U.S. Bureau of the Census: *Population Trends in the U.S.: 1900 to 1960*, technical paper no. 10, Washington, D.C., 1964.

U.S. Department of Commerce: *Current Populations Reports—Consumer Income*, series P-60, no. 82, July 1972, Washington, D.C.

Vanden Berghe, P.: *Race and Racism*, Wiley, New York, 1967.

Valentine, C.: *Culture and Poverty: Critique and Counter-proposals*, University of Chicago Press, Chicago, 1968.

Valentine, C.: "Deficit, Difference, and Bicultural Models of Afro-American Behavior," *Harvard Educational Review*, 41:137–157, 1971.

Ward, L. M., R. D. Ashmore, and D. A. Wexler: "Some Psychological Principles in the Design of Multi- and Single-Family Dwelling Units,"

The State of New Jersey Department of Community Affairs Division of Housing and Urban Renewal, 1972.

Wayson, W. W.: "Expressed Motives of Teachers in Slum Schools," *Urban Education,* 1:222–238, 1965.

Wilkerson, D. A.: "Compensatory Education," in S. Marcus and H. Rivlin (eds.), *Conflicts in Urban Education,* Basic Books, New York, 1970, pp. 19–39.

Will, R. E., and H. G. Vater (eds.): *Poverty in Affluence,* Harcourt, Brace and World, New York, 1970.

Williams, F. (ed.): *Language and Poverty,* Markham Publishing Co., Chicago, 1970.

Winsborough, H. H.: "The Social Consequences of High Population Density," *Law and Contemporary Problems,* 30:120–126, 1955.

Wirth, L.: "Urbanism As a Way of Life," in J. Tager and P. D. Goist (eds.), *The Urban Vision: Selected Interpretations of the Modern American City,* Dorsey Press, Homewood, Ill., 1970, pp. 116–130.

Wittes, S.: *People and Power,* Center for Research on Utilization of Scientific Knowledge, Ann Arbor, Mich., 1970.

Wrightsman, L. S.: *Social Psychology in the Seventies,* Brooks-Cole, Monterey, Calif., 1972.

Zawadski, B., and P. Lazarsfeld: "The Psychological Consequences of Unemployment," *Journal of Social Psychology,* 6:224–251, 1935.

Zellman, G. L., and D. O. Sears: "Childhood Origins of Tolerance for Dissent," *Journal of Social Issues,* 27:109–136, 1971.

Name Index

Subject Index